Legal Almanac Series No. 65

ENVIRONMENT

AND

THE LAW

By
Irving J. Sloan, J.D.,

.

1971
OCEANA PUBLICATIONS, INC.
Dobbs Ferry, New York

Library of Congress Catalog Card Number: 79-156377

International Standard Book Number: 0-379-11077-6

Manufactured in the United States of America

To Marie Ricci and Robert Baum,
teacher and student who lead
in the quest for environmental quality.

CONTENTS

PREFACE

The year 1970 marked the first year of what is likely to be characterized by historians as the Decade of the Environment. While the year may not have heralded a change in the quality of the environment, it certainly marked the beginning of a new emphasis on the environment so that change before the end of the decade is inevitable.

So monumental is the weight of concern of the public in the environment and pollution that law and legislation have emerged dealing with it to a degree almost unparalleled in legal and legislative history, given the short period of time which has passed since environmental quality has become a household word in America.

Though environmental problems are indeed old, their complexity and potential enormity are so vast that present law and legislation and methods of control are still in the early stages of their development. While a body of environmental law is indeed developing at perhaps a breath-taking pace, much of it remains tentative or at least pending. Traditional theories of law are still relevant, but for how long is questionable. This is by way of reminding the reader of this volume that he must constantly turn to the most current literature and reports before making any conclusions or taking any steps suggested by the comments and issues which appear here!

Environmental control problems are of such a nature that we cannot be strictly concerned with the law. The problems are such that their social, economic and political aspects must be considered before one can fully come to grips with the legal and administrative problems. Hence the reader will find considerable "extra-"legal discussion in these pages. Much of this, incidentally, has been drawn from The First Annual Report of the Council on Environmental Quality, Environmental Quality, transmitted to the Congress August, 1970.

For the practicing attorney there is a growing and impressive literature dealing with environmental law. Our survey here is designed, hopefully, to give the general reader some basic background of the legal aspects of the great hope and aspiration of the present decade: environmental quality.

May, 1971   Irving J. Sloan

THE STRUCTURE OF
FEDERAL ENVIRONMENT CONTROL

In May 1969, President Richard M. Nixon established the first organizational entity charged with taking a broad overview of environmental problems--the Cabinet-level Environmental Quality Council, chaired by the President. It was still felt, however, that the Executive Office needed an independent organization concerned exclusively with environmental problems and yet not made up of the many existing agencies. Such an organization would be free to look at the environmental problems in new ways and to propose new approaches to dealing with them. Congress enacted two related measures: the National Environmental Policy Act of 1969 and the Environmental Quality Improvement Act of 1970. The Cabinet-level Environmental Quality Council was abolished and a Domestic Council in the Executive Office of the President was established.

On January 1, 1970, President Nixon signed the National Environmental Policy Act (Public Law 91-190). That act established a national policy on the environment, placed new responsibilities on Federal agencies to take environmental factors into account in their decisionmaking, and created a Council on Environmental Quality in the Executive Office of the President.

The act charges the Council with assisting the President in preparing an annual environmental quality report and making recommendations to him on national policies for improving environmental quality. It empowers the Council to analyze conditions and trends in the quality of the environment and to conduct investigations relating to the environment. It gives the Council responsibility for appraising the effect of Federal programs and activities on environmental quality, and authorizes funds for 1970-1973.

The Council's ability to perform its functions was significantly strengthened by the Environmental Quality Improvement Act of 1970 (Public Law 91-224), which was passed as Title II of the Water Quality Improvement Act of 1970. This act created a new Office of Environmental Quality, which provides staff support to the Council. The Chairman of the Council of Environmental Quality serves as its Director and the activities of the Council and Office are meshed into one entity. The Environmental Quality Improvement Act also added to the responsibilities of the Council and the Office. It specified that they should review monitoring, evaluate the effects of technology, and assist Federal agencies in the development of environmental standards.

On March 5, 1970, the President issued Executive Order 11514. Together with the two public laws, it empowers the Council to recommend to the President and to Federal agencies priorities in environmental programs. Under the order and the acts, the Council will also promote the development and use of indices and monitoring systems and advise and assist the President and the agencies in achieving international environmental cooperation-- under the foreign policy guidance of the Department of State. Taken together, the legislation and the Executive Order provide a broad charter for the Council. They also provide a mandate for reform in the wat Federal agencies make environmental decisions --from initial planning to implementation.

The National Environmental Policy Act of 1969 (NEPA) will probably prove to be the most important piece of environmental legislation ever written. It requires Federal agencies to take several significant steps. One is to include in every recommendation or report on legislation and on other major Federal actions significantly affecting the quality of the environment a detailed statement concerning the environmental impact of the action, adverse impacts that cannot be avoided, alternatives to the proposed action, the relationship between short- and long-term uses, and any irreversible commitment of resources involved. The detailed statements will include the comments of State and local environmental agencies as well as appropriate Federal agencies with environmental expertise. The statements will then be made available to the Council on Environmental Quality, the President and the public.

Executive Order 11514 further requires that Federal agencies continually monitor their own activities to enhance environmental quality. The order also requires that the agencies provide for timely public information and hearings, where appropriate, on Federal plans and programs with potential environmental impact.

On April 30, 1970, the Council on Environmental Quality issued Interim Guidelines for the preparation of environmental statements, requiring each Federal agency to establish internal procedures for implementing this provision of the act. The Council's Interim Guidelines, published in the Federal Register, will be reivewed and revised as necessary.

In addition to its immediate impact within the Federal establishment, the provision of the law requiring detailed environmental statements has been the subject of litigation in several lawsuits and administrative proceedings. In one instance, a Federal court blocked a Federal loan to develop a wildlife habitat into a golf course pending submission of the required environmental analysis. In another, the Corps of Engineers was enjoined from removing the ground cover along a river in Arizona.

The environmental statements required of the agencies add a vital step to the decisionmaking process. Federal agencies are now required to consider explicitly the environmental implications of their actions. Such considerations will permit Federal, State and local agencies and other Federal agencies having an interest in the environment to review the environmental implications of a Federal project before the project is undertaken. The Federal government need no longer be in the position of trying to repair damage to the environment after the damage has been done because the relevant factors were not considered at the time of the decision.

The courts have indicated that they intend to follow the Congressional mandate to interpret Federal policies, regulations and statutes in accordance with the statutory national policy of protecting environmental quality. In one case the court commented strongly on the importance of construing the provisions of the National Environmental Policy Act in favor of the environment:

> The Congress has expressed in strong and clear language their concern over what we are doing to our environment. In the language of the statute, Congress has recognized the 'critical importance of restoring and maintaining environmental quality . . . .' It is hard to imagine a clearer or stronger mandate to the courts.

On the strength of this interpretation of NEPA, the court granted a stay pending appeal to prevent the Farmers Home Administration from expanding funds on a construction project whose environmental effects had not been considered under the provisions of NEPA. The court noted the case would become moot if the stay were denied, because construction damage could not be undone. It also found that the plaintiff had a reasonable chance of success in its injunction action and that the plaintiff's allegations of possible environmental ill effects were sufficient. In another case, the court granted a preliminary injunction forbidding the Secretary of the Interior from issuing a permit for the construction of the trans-Alaska pipeline and access road, in part, because he did not comply with the requirements of NEPA.

AIR POLLUTION

Process and Causes

Five main classes of pollutants are pumped into the air over the United States, totaling more than 200 million tons per year.

Transportation--particularly the automobile--is the greatest source of air pollution. It accounts for 42 per cent of all pollutants by weight. It produces major portions not only of carbon monoxide but of hydrocarbons and nitrogen oxides.

Carbon monoxide (CO) is a colorless, odorless, poisonous gas, slightly lighter than air, that is produced by the incomplete burning of the carbon in fuels. Carbon monoxide emissions can be prevented by supplying enough air to insure complete combustion. When this occurs, carbon dioxide, a natural constituent of the atmosphere, is produced instead of carbon monoxide. In American cities, the primary source of this gas is the automobile.

Particulate matter includes particles of solid or liquid substances in a very wide range of sizes, from those that are visible as soot and smoke to particles too small to detect except under an electron microscope. Particulates may be so small that they remain in the air for long periods and can be transported great distances by the winds. They are produced primarily by stationary fuel combustion (31 per cent) and industrial processes (27 per cent). Forest fires and other miscellaneous sources account for 34 per cent.

There are established techniques for controlling particulates from a boiler stack or from a waste air stream--among them filtering, washing, centrifugal separation and electrostatic precipitation. These work well for most of the particles, but complete removal, especially of the very finest particles, is technically and economically difficult.

Sulfur oxides (SO_x) are acrid, corrosive, poisonous gases produced when fuel containing sulfur is burned. Electric utilities and industrial plants are its principal producers, since their most abundant fuels are coal and oil, which contain sulfur as an impurity. The burning of coal produces about 60 per cent of all sulfur oxides emissions, oil about 14 per cent, and industrial processes that use sulfur 22 per cent. Most of the coal and oil is burned in electric power generation plants. About two-thirds of the nation's sulfur oxides are emitted in urban areas, where industry and population are concentrated. And seven industrial States in the Northeast account for almost half of the national total of sulfur oxides. In rural areas, however, sulfur oxide sources may be large industrial plants, smelters or power plants. Any one of these may throw out several hundred thousand tons of sulfur oxides in a year.

Government agencies and industry have sought to reduce sulfur oxide emissions in three ways: switching to low sulfur fuels (those with less than 1 per cent sulfur), removing sulfur from fuels entirely, and removing sulfur oxides from the combustion gases.

Hydrocarbons (HC), like carbon monoxide, represent unburned and wasted fuel. Unlike carbon monoxide, gaseous hydrocarbons at concentrations normally found in the atmosphere are not toxic, but they are a major pollutant because of their role in forming photochemical smog. More than half the estimated 32 million tons of hydrocarbons produced each year comes from transportation sources, mainly gasoline-fueled vehicles. Another 27 per cent comes from miscellaneous burning and 14 per cent from industrial processes. About 60 per cent is produced in urban areas, largely because there are more automobiles.

Nitrogen oxides (NO_x) are produced when fuel is burned at very high temperatures. Stationary combustion plants produce 49 per cent of the nitrogen oxide emissions; transportation vehicles, 39 per cent; and all other sources, 12 per cent.

Internal combustion engines operate at very high temperatures, and so do efficient, large electric power and industrial boilers. Nitrogen that is ordinarily inert combines with oxygen in high temperature flames and tends to stay combined if the exhaust gases are cooled too quickly. The control of NO_x from stationary sources requires careful adjustment of flame and stack gas temperatures. Control of nitrogen oxides from automobiles is more difficult because reducing other pollutants can increase the output of NO_x.

Under the influence of sunlight, nitrogen oxides combine with gaseous hydrocarbons to form a complex variety of secondary pollutants called photochemical oxidants. These oxidants, together with solid and liquid particles in the air, make up what is commonly known as smog. The photochemical oxidant family of pollutants includes, among others, ozone, an unstable, toxic form of oxygen; nitrogen dioxide; peroxyacyl nitrates; aldehydes; and acrolein. In air they can cause eye and lung irritation, damage to vegetation, offensive odor, and thick haze.

Air pollution adversely affects man and his environment in many ways. It soils his home and interferes with the growth of plants and shrubs. It diminishes the value of his agricultural products. It obscures his view and adds unpleasant smells to his environment. Most important, it endangers his health. Acute episodes of pollution in London, New York, and other cities have been marked by dramatic increases in death and illness rates, especially among the elderly and those with preexisting respiratory or cardiac conditions.

The total costs of air pollution in the United States cannot be precisely calculated, but they amount to many billions of dollars a year. Economic studies are beginning to identify some of the more obvious costs. To paint steel structures damaged by air pollution runs an estimated $100 million a year. Commercial laundering, cleaning and dyeing of fabrics soiled by air pollution costs about $240 million. Damage to agricultural crops and livestock is put at $500 million a year or more. Adverse effects of air pollution on air travel cost from $40 to $80 million a year. Even more difficult to tie down are the costs of replacing and protecting precision instruments or maintaining cleanliness in the production of foods, beverages and other comsumables.

It is equally difficult to assess damage, soiling and added maintenance to homes and furnishings or how air pollution acts on property values. The cost of fuels wasted in incomplete combustion and of valuable and potentially recoverable resources such as sulfur wasted into the air is also hard to count. It is still more difficult to determine the dollar value of medical costs and time lost from work because of air pollution--or to calculate the resulting fall in productivity of business and industry.

7

Legislative Control

The first Federal legislation concerned exclusively with air pollution was enacted in July 1955. It authorized $5 million annually to the Public Health Service of the Department of Health, Education and Welfare for research, data collection, and technical assistance to State and local governments.

Pressures for action led to the Clean Air Act of 1963. It provided grants to air pollution agencies for control programs (with special bonuses for intermunicipal or interstate areas). And it provided Federal enforcement authority to attack interstate air pollution problems.

In October 1965, the Clean Air Act was amended to permit national regulation of air pollution from new motor vehicles. The first standards were applied to 1968 models. These standards were tightened for 1970 and 1971 model cars. And even more stringent standards have been announced for 1973 and 1975.

In November 1965, the Congress passed the comprehensive Air Quality Act, which undergirds much of the current Federal air pollution control effort. That act set in motion a new regional approach to establishing and enforcing Federal-State air quality standards:

> The Secretary of HEW first must designate air quality control regions within a state or within an interstate region.
>
> The Secretary must promulgate air quality criteria which, based on scientific studies, describe the harmful effects of an air pollutant on health, vegetation, and materials. He must issue control technology documents showing availability, costs and effectiveness of prevention and control techniques.
>
> In the designated regions, the states must show willingness to establish air quality standards. The states then set standards limiting the levels of the pollutant described in the criteria and control technology documents. If the states fail to do this, the Secretary is empowered to set the standards.

After the states have developed air quality standards, they must establish comprehensive plans for implementing them. (These plans should set specific emission levels by source and a timetable for achieving compliance.)

The process of adopting standards and implementation plans can take up to a year and a half, and the approval process requires still more time. The process must be renewed and repeated each time criteria and control techniques are issued for a new pollutant.

Thus it is clear that the procedures for establishing air quality standards are replete with conferences, hearings and delays. The conference-public hearing procedure has been a cumbersome and time-consuming method of taking action against individual polluters. The first air pollution enforcement action was instituted in 1965 against a chicken-rendering plant in Bishop, Maryland. A conference was held in 1965 and a public hearing in 1967; a suit was begun in the Federal district court in 1969, and an appeal finally made to the U.S. Supreme Court. The plant was not shut down until the Supreme Court refused to hear the appeal in May 1970--5 years after the action started. No other enforcement action has proceeded beyond the conference stage. No enforcement has yet taken place under the 1967 Act, since the standards, for the most part, have not yet been adopted nor implementation plans approved.

The Department of Health, Education and Welfare is required to, and has, prescribed standards for emissions from new cars and engines. New cars and engines must meet these standards unless they are intended solely for export, or are otherwise exempted by HEW. Violations may be enjoined and violators fined. The act preempts state emission controls, except that this provision may be and has been waived annually for California on the basis of California's stricter standards. Under the National Emission Standards Act, HEW may make grants to state air pollution control agencies to develop inspection and testing programs. In addition, it may and has required registration of fuel additives.

The legal theories which may be utilized by private parties in private litigation in air pollution cases are, generally speaking, the traditional torts--nuisance, trespass, and negligence. The

9

greatest difficulty facing private litigants seeking recovery or relief in air pollution cases is the situation wherein the pollution has passed from a single identifiable source such as a factory chimney to that of a community-wide pollution resulting from the conmingling of pollutants from single point sources to spread over a wide area. At this stage private litigation is rarely feasible because of the difficulties in establishing causation and identifying the tortfeasor.

III

WATER POLLUTION

Process and Causes

Throughout history man has been ravaged by plague and epidemics visited him by poor sanitation and polluted water. In more modern times, the great typhoid epidemics that swept London in the mid-19th century underscored the peril of water pollution and launched the first organized steps to combat it. And until recent times this stress on preventing waterborne disease was the major thrust of efforts to stem the decline of the environment.

Americans have acted, until recently, as though their rivers and lakes had an infinite capacity to absorb wastes. Pollution was considered the price of progress. Not until 1948 was comprehensive Federal water pollution control legislation enacted, and the first permanent legislation was not passed until 1956. The original overriding concern was with human health, and almost all State water pollution programs were carried out by State health departments.

Water pollution control legislation and programs have now been broadened to embrace a host of environmental concerns, including recreation and esthetics. Epidemics due to waterborne causes are largely of the past, and our health efforts have moved to a more sophisticated concern for the effects of small amounts of toxic chemicals on humans and other forms of life.

Pollution problems exist in all parts of the United States, particularly in the Northeast and in the Great Lakes region. In these areas, which have experienced tremendous urban and industrial growth over the past century, there was, at least until recently, inadequate investment in the construction of treatment plants. Now a big backlog of needed construction has accumulated. Specific sources of pollution, besides the ordinary municipal and industrial wastes, affect certain areas. Acid mine pollution is common in the coal mining states of Appalachia, and saline pollution occurs in the irrigation areas of Western states.

Several basic biological, chemical and physical processes affect the quality of water.

Organic wastes decompose by bacterial action. Bacteria attack wastes dumped into rivers and lakes, using up oxygen in the process. Organic wastes are measured in units of biochemical oxygen demand (BOD), or chemical oxygen demand (COD), both measures of the amount of oxygen needed to decompose them. The COD measure is more inclusive than BOD, but BOD is much more commonly used. Fish and other aquatic life need oxygen. If the waste loads are so great that large amounts of oxygen are spent in their decomposition, certain types of fish can no longer live in that body of water. A pollution resistant, lower order of fish, such as carp, replace the original fish population. The amount of oxygen in a water body is therefore one of the best measures of its ecological health.

If all the oxygen is used, an anaerobic (without air) decomposition process is set in motion with a different mixture of bacteria. Rather than releasing carbon dioxide in the decomposition process, anaerobic decomposition releases methane, or hydrogen sulfide. In these highly polluted situations, the river turns dark, and odors--often overwhelming--penetrate the environment.

Heated water discharged into lakes and rivers often harms aquatic life. Heat accelerates biological and chemical processes, which reduce the ability of a body of water to retain dissolved oxygen and other dissolved gases. Increases in temperature often disrupt the reproduction cycles of fish. By hastening biological processes, heat accelerates the growth of aquatic plants--often algae. Finally, the temperature level determines the types of fish and other aquatic life that can live in any particular body of water. Taken together, these effects of excess heat operate to change the ecology of an area--sometimes drastically and rapidly.

One of the most serious water pollution problems is eutrophication--the "dying of lakes." All lakes go through a natural cycle of eutrophication, but normally it takes thousands of years. In the first stage--the oligotrophic--lakes are deep and have little biological life. Lake Superior is a good example. Over time, nutrients and sediments are added; the lake becomes more biologically productive and shallower. This stage--the mesotrophic--has been reached by Lake Ontario. As nutrients change and the lake begins to take on undesirable characteristics, the eutrophic stage is reached. Lake Erie is now in this eutrophic stage. Over time the lake becomes a swamp and finally a land area.

Man greatly accelerates this process of eutrophication when he adds nutrients to the water--detergents, fertilizers, and human wastes. He has done this in Lake Erie and countless other lakes. Man's action can, in decades, cause changes that would have taken nature thousands of years.

Although water pollution comes from many sources, the major ones are industrial, municipal and agricultural.

The more than 300, 000 water-using factories in the United States discharge three to four times as much oxygen-demanding wastes as all the sewered population of the United States. Moreover, many of the wastes discharged by industry are toxic. The output of industrial wastes is growing several times faster than the volume of sanitary sewage.

Although there is no detailed inventory of industrial wastes, indications are that over half the volume discharged to water comes from four major industry groups--paper, organic chemicals, petroleum and steel.

The greatest volume of industrial wastes is discharged in the Northeast, the Ohio River Basin, the Great Lakes, and the Gulf Coast States. Lesser but significant volumes are discharged in some areas of the Southeast and the Pacific Coast States.

Municipal waste treatment plants handle more than just domestic wastes from homes and apartments. On a nationwide average, about 55 per cent of the wastes processed by municipal treatment plants comes from homes and commercial establishments and about 45 per cent from industries. Less than one-third of the nation's population is served by a system of sewers and an adequate treatment plant. About one-third is not served by a sewer system at all. About 5 per cent is served by sewers which discharge their wastes without any treatment. And the remaining 32 per cent have sewers but inadequate treatment plants. Of the total sewered population, about 60 per cent have adequate treatment systems. The greatest municipal waste problems exist in the areas with the heaviest concentrations of population, particularly the Northeast.

Wastes from feedlots are a key source of agricultural pollution. The increasing number of animals and modern methods of raising them contribute to the worsening pollution of waters

13

by animal wastes. Beef cattle, poultry and swine feeding operations, along with dairy farms, are the major sources of actual or potential water pollution from animal wastes. Animal wastes are estimated to be the equivalent of the wastes of 2 billion people. These figures should not be interpreted as an estimate of the potential pollution from feedlots, however, since most of these wastes never reach the water. But they are a measure of the total amount of animal wastes, part of which causes water pollution and solid waste problems.

Sediments carried by erosion represent the greatest volume of wastes entering surface waters. The volume of suspended solids reaching U.S. waters is at least 700 times greater than the total sewage discharge loadings. Sediments are washed in from croplands, unprotected forest soils, overgrazed pastures, strip mines, roads or bulldozed urban areas. Agricultural development increases land erosion rates four to nine times over what they are for natural cover. Construction may increase the rate a hundredfold.

With the grounding of the Torrey Canyon in 1967, the breakup of the Ocean Eagle in Puerto Rican waters in 1968, and the Santa Barbara offshore oil leak in 1969, oil pollution has become recognized as a serious national and world-wide problem. An estimated 10,000 spills of oil and other hazardous materials annually pollute navigable waters of the United States. Although damages from other hazardous substances can be just as significant and diverse as those caused by oil pollution, the volume of oil transported and used makes it the most important single pollutant of this type.

Most oil spills exceeding 100 barrels come from vessels, although about one-third of the incidents involve pipelines, oil terminals and bulk storage facilities. Vessel casualties are a prime source of oil pollution.

Oil pollution may spring from several other sources. Gasoline service stations dispose of 350 million gallons of used oil per year, much of which was previously refined. Two hundred thousand miles of pipelines, carrying more than a billion tons of oil and hazardous substances across waterways and reservoirs and are subject to leakage. The blowout of offshore oil and gas wells, the dumping of drilling muds and oil-soaked wastes, the destruction of offshore rigs by storms, and ship collisions--all are significant potential sources of pollution.

14

Mine drainage is one of the most significant sources of water pollution in Appalachia, in the Ohio Basin states, and in certain other areas of the country. Acid formation occurs when water and air react with the sulfur-bearing minerals in the mines or in refuse piles to form sulfuric acid and iron compounds. Coal mines idle for 30 to 50 years may still discharge large quantities of acid waters. Mine drainage also contains copper, lead, zinc and other metals toxic to aquatic life.

Legislative Control

The first temporary water pollution control legislation was passed in 1948. Permanent legislation was enacted in 1956. The Federal Water Pollution Control Act of 1956 authorized planning, technical assistance, grants for state programs and construction grants for municipal waste treatment facilities. Amendments followed in 1961 which, among other things, extended Federal enforcement authority and increased construction grant authorization.

In 1965, more amendments established the Federal Water Pollution Control Administration as successor to a program previously in the Public Health Service of the Department of Health, Education and Welfare. It provides for the establishment of water quality standards and plans for their implementation and enforcement by the states or by the Secretary of Interior with regard to interstate waters, but not merely navigable waters. The standards must "protect the public health or welfare, enhance the quality of water and serve the purpose of /this Act/." In establishing standards, the use and value of water for public water supplies, the propagation of fish and wildlife, recreational purposes, and agricultural, industrial and other legitimate uses must be considered.

The Clean Water Restoration Act of 1966 provided more Federal money for building treatment facilities. The Water Quality Improvement Act of 1970 gives a new name to the responsible agency, the Federal Water Quality Administration; provides tighter controls over oil pollution, vessel pollution, and pollution from federal activities; and broadens the earlier laws in other respects.

The states are the primary enforcers of water quality standards. If they fail to act, the Secretary of the Interior may then set standards and enforce them. The standards of all the states have now been approved. The goal--to provide nationwide, comprehensive water quality standards--however, is far from reached. Over half the states established standards that were not stringent enough in all aspects to assure adequate water quality protection. For example, the temperature criteria of a number of states have been excepted because they did not set adequate safeguards against thermal pollution. In some cases implementation plans have not been approved because the abatement measures or the schedules were deemed inadequate.

The complicated enforcement mechanism of the Act is largely responsible for the ineffectiveness of Federal efforts thus far. The procedure begins with a conference that may be called by the Secretary of the Interior when he has reason to believe water pollution is crossing state lines. If the pollution is entirely intrastate, he may not act unless so requested by the governor of the state. The conference is attended by appropriate state water pollution authorities; those contributing to or affected by the pollution may recommend remedial action to the appropriate state authority, but he may then take no further enforcement action for six months. The next step is a public hearing by a hearing board appointed by the Secretary. If the hearing board concludes pollution is occurring, it may recommend that the Secretary order abatement within a reasonable time (no less than six months). Finally, if there is still no progress toward abatement, the Secretary may ask the Department of Justice to bring an action to abate the pollution. The consent of the governor is needed for a suit dealing with intrastate pollution.

The standard for judicial review is requiring the court de novo to give " . . . due consideration to the practicability and to the physical and economic feasibility of complying with such standards."

The Federal water pollution control program, as embodied in the Water Pollution Control Act, fails to achieve its goals for a number of reasons. While the Act's policy is to encourage state pollution abatement efforts, it fails to recognize that water pollution problems are typically interstate, so that a measure of national coordination is necessary. The most important defect in tha Act is the inadequate enforcement provisions. The interminable conferences and hearings required by the Act make enforcement proceedings unfeasible. Since 1948 when the first water pollution control legislation was enacted, there have been only two abatement proceedings under the Control Act.

It is always a source of amazement to view the Refuse Act, or more properly, Section 13 of the Rivers and Harbors Act of 1899, as a 19th century piece of legislation. It makes unlawful to discharge "any refuse matter of any kind or description whatever other than that flowing from streets and sewers and passing therefrom in a liquid state" into any navigable water of the United States, except as authorized by the Secretary of the Army. This Act is still fully alive and has in no way been replaced by the Federal Water Pollution Control Act. Section 16 of the Act makes violation of Section 13 a misdemeanor. Fines may not exceed $2,500, nor may they be less than $500 per violation. Imprisonment may not be for less than 30 days nor for more than 1 year. Both fines and imprisonment may be imposed and for the same violation. "Violation" under the Refuse Act is undefined, but it arguably applies to each separate day of discharge. The United States is not limited to the inadequate criminal penalties and may bring a civil action to enjoin unlawful discharges.

Although the courts have looked favorably on prosecutions brought under the Refuse Act of 1899, enforcement proceedings have been rare. This in spite of the statement in the Act that it is the "duty of the United States attorneys to vigorously prosecute all offenders" of the Refuse Act. However, the Justice Department has only recently indicated that the government would not prosecute firms that were discharging refuse but were spending "significant amounts of money" to abate pollution under a plan approved by the Federal Water Quality Administration. This statement was in response to criticism from members of Congress and conservation groups.

In any event, the reluctance of the government to act has prompted citizens' suits to enforce the Act, with the citizens collecting half of any penalty imposed. The Rivers and Harbors Act provides that a person who gives information leading to a conviction may collect one half of the fine. The Supreme Court has held that when a statute provides a reward or bounty for a citizen who informs on violators, he may bring a civil action in the name of the United States to collect the sum to which the statute entitles him. Such suits are called qui tam suits.

It is encouraging to note that the Corps of Engineers has announced that it will begin to require permits for construction of sewage outfalls or cooling water or outfall structures "which may

17

effect the navigable capacity and/or the ecology of a waterway." Applicants must furnish data on the chemical content of discharges, water temperature differentials, toxicity, and type and quantity of solids. The applicant must also furnish plans for pollution abatement. These are regulations which appear under "Regulation No. 1145-2-303."

Private complainants must generally bring their actions in water pollution cases on the theory of nuisance. Such nuisance must be shown to be an unreasonable, nontrespassory interference with the use and enjoyment of an interest in land. The plaintiff in nuisance actions must show that he has suffered a private harm. But if he is suffering only as a member of the general public, then such public nuisance may be abated only by a public official. The plaintiff, in order to show private harm, must show that his damages are different in kind and degree from those of the general public. There is the further problem of recovering for aesthetic as distinguished from actual physical damages. There is an encouraging trend in the courts to consider specific aesthetic offense as a cause of recovery in a private water pollution action, but there has been no such holding as yet. The most common defenses to nuisance actions are the statute of limitations and claims of prescriptive rights to pollute.

While riparian owners have a right to be assured that their water retains a minimum degree of quality, how much quality depends on whether the courts follow the "natural flow" doctrine which holds that landowners whose land touches a watercourse are entitled to have such stream flow naturally, undiminished and unpolluted, subject only to right to withdraw water for "natural uses," or whether the court employs the "reasonable use" theory, which permits a "reasonable" amount of pollution. Generally, when the "reasonable use" theory is offered as the test, the courts have held that an individual's inconvenience must give way to the assumed public interest in individual productivity.

The Oil Pollution Act of 1946 has been repealed by the 1970 Amendments to the Federal Water Pollution Control Act.

> Section 11 (b) (1) The Congress hereby declares that it is in the policy of the United States that there should be no discharges of oil into or upon the navigable waters of the United States, adjoining

shorelines, or into or upon the waters of the contiguous zone.

Thus Section 11 of the Water Quality Improvement Act prohibits the dumping of oil in the navigable waters of the United States
and provides for fines up to $10,000 against anyone knowingly dis-
charging oil into the water or anyone failing to notify promptly
any discharge.

> Section 11 (b) (4) Any person in charge of a ves-
> sel or of an onshore facility shall, as soon as he
> has knowledge of any discharge of oil from such
> vessel or facility in violation of paragraph (2) of
> this subsection, immediately notify the appropriate
> agency of the United States Government of such
> discharge. Any such person who fails to notify
> immediately such agency of such discharge, shall,
> upon conviction, be fined not more than $10,000,
> or imprisoned for not more than one year, or both.
> Notification received pursuant to this paragraph
> or information obtained by the exploitation of such
> notification shall not be used against any such per-
> son in any criminal case, except a prosecution
> for perjury or for giving a false statement.

Section 11 also establishes a National Contingency Plan for
the immediate clean-up of oil spills with responsibility vested
directly in the President. Under this Plan the United States may
coordinate all clean-up activities. In case of emergency the President may require the U.S. District Attorney in the area to seek
the necessary relief in Federal district courts. The district courts
have jurisdiction to grant "such relief as the public interest and
the equities of the case may require."

Liability for oil spills holds that the owner or operator of a
vessel or an onshore or offshore facility will be liable at least for
the cost of removing or dispersing the oil, unless he can prove the
discharge was caused solely by an act of God, an act of war, negligence on the part of the United States, or an act of omission of
a third party, regardless of his negligence. This Section does
not effect the liability for damage to public or private property
from the discharge or removal of any oil.

19

IV

NOISE POLLUTION

Decibels and Noisemakers

Noise is everywhere, especially in urban areas, where three-fourths of the nation lives. The roar of air and surface transportation, the general din and hum of construction projects, and industrial noise all pound against the ear virtually without ceasing. In the decade of the 1960's, the measured amounts and extent of urban noise rose significantly. And so did the social awareness of noise and the discomfort caused by it.

Urban dwellers cannot escape it. They are surrounded by a multitude of noise sources in homes, offices or places of work. Even at play they are bombarded by scores of outdoor noises.

The most severe noise conditions are generally encountered in the work environment. Excessive exposure to such noise for long periods is known to cause irreversible hearing loss. It is estimated that up to 16 million American workers today are threatened with hearing damage.

Traffic noise in a modern city may reach 90 decibels. A decibel is a logarithmic measure of sound. Because it is logarithmic, linear comparisons of decibel levels cannot be made. For example, a noise pressure level of 130 decibels is 10 times as great as one of 120 decibels and 100 times as great as a noise pressure level of 110 decibels. It is widely accepted that steady exposure to about 90 decibels can cause permanent hearing loss.

In general, trucks, buses, motorcycles and rail systems are the worst offenders. For example, at expressway speeds a single trailer truck can generate steady noise levels above 90 decibels. A line of trucks can produce noise levels of 100 decibels or more.

The rapid growth of aviation since World War II and the development of jets have created a major noise problem in airports and the areas around them. A four-engine jet at takeoff generates 115 to 120 decibels. The Airport Operators Council International estimates that by 1975, 15 million people will be living near enough to airports to be subjected to intense aircraft noise. These people will be regularly subjected to the extreme noise of huge airplanes taking off or landing. Those who bear these constant invasions are probably the country's most vociferous opponents of noise pollution. Over the last 20 years the bulk of the legal action in the field of noise pollution has been on the complaint of home-owners' associations and pressure groups residing near airports.

The development of the Supersonic Transport (SST), if it follows the lines currently anticipated by its supporters, will surely result in a tremendous increase in the number of persons offended by noise pollution.

Noise can have many adverse effects, including damage to hearing, disruption of normal activity and general annoyance. Extremely loud noise, such as a sonic boom, can also cause physical damage to structures.

Although many noise problems are inherently local, the Federal Government has taken the leadership in the fight to combat unnecessary noise. Among the steps it has taken in this direction are:

> 1. The Department of Labor, in May 1969, issued the first Federal standards for occupational exposure to noise.
>
> 2. The Department of Transportation, in November 1969, issued the first of a series of noise standards under Public Law 90-411 regulating aircraft noise. In April 1970, the Department issued a proposed rule banning overland flights of supersonic transports.
>
> 3. In late 1969, the First Federal Aircraft Noise Abatement Plan was published summarizing the overall program for airport noise research and development.
>
> 4. The Department of Housing and Urban Development (HUD) is preparing to issue a policy circular. It will set uniform policy and lay down interim

Weighted Sound Levels and Human Response

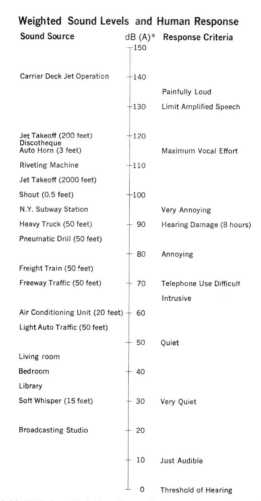

Weighted Sound Levels and Human Response

Sound Source	dB (A)*	Response Criteria
	┌─150	
Carrier Deck Jet Operation	┼─140	
		Painfully Loud
	┼─130	Limit Amplified Speech
Jet Takeoff (200 feet)	┼─120	
Discotheque		
Auto Horn (3 feet)		Maximum Vocal Effort
Riveting Machine	┼─110	
Jet Takeoff (2000 feet)		
Shout (0.5 feet)	┼─100	
N.Y. Subway Station		Very Annoying
Heavy Truck (50 feet)	┼─ 90	Hearing Damage (8 hours)
Pneumatic Drill (50 feet)		
	┼─ 80	Annoying
Freight Train (50 feet)		
Freeway Traffic (50 feet)	┼─ 70	Telephone Use Difficult
		Intrusive
Air Conditioning Unit (20 feet)	┼─ 60	
Light Auto Traffic (50 feet)		
	┼─ 50	Quiet
Living room		
Bedroom	┼─ 40	
Library		
Soft Whisper (15 feet)	┼─ 30	Very Quiet
Broadcasting Studio	┼─ 20	
	┼─ 10	Just Audible
	└─ 0	Threshold of Hearing

*Typical A—Weighted sound levels taken with a sound-level meter and expressed as decibels on the scale. The "A" scale approximates the frequency response of the human ear.
Source: Department of Transportation.

standards of noise exposure that HUD will use to determine if proposed housing sites are suitable.

5. The National Aeronautics and Space Administration in 1969 successfully demonstrated that new technology could be applied to cut down noise in current jet aircraft. Such research continues. In 1970 NASA was authorized to construct a new acoustics laboratory to conduct advanced research on aircraft noise.

State and local governments play a major role in legislating and enforcing noise control strategies. Most states, for example, have statutes or codes relating to muffler noise on motor vehicles. But the laws usually fail to spell out enforcement techniques and maximum noise levels. Hence, these regulations are almost impossible to enforce. In 1965, New York became the first state to enact a state highway anti-noise statute. In 1967, California enacted an even more comprehensive statute. Its new highway anti-noise statute specifies maximum permissible noise levels for passenger cars, trucks, buses, and motorcycles and prescribes levels and test procedures as a requisite for new vehicle sales.

Private actions resulting from property loss, personal injury, or emotional pain, against noise polluters may proceed on one or more of three theories: (1) inverse condemnation or "taking of property." The landmark case dealt with noise of overflying aircraft which essentially destroyed the residential value of a plaintiff's land and its beneficial use as a commercial chicken farm. Relief was granted on the theory of inverse condemnation, holding that the noise of defendant's airplanes was an invasion of plaintiff's land and a taking of property without just compensation in violation of the Fifth Amendment. This theory of inverse condemnation has become the most likely basis for recovery for noise pollution. But the application of inverse condemnation may be limited to cases in which the taking is a physical trespass by aircraft flying directly over the plaintiff's property.

(2) Private actions in tort may be pursued on traditional theories. While in the usual case fault must be shown, the noisemaker may be held strictly liable where it is proved that the noise

23

was an ultrahazardous activity, such as blasting. Negligence may be inferred by a violation of statutory standard, such as a rule requiring minimum flying altitudes.

(3) Common law nuisance is another basis for recovery. Here the weighing of the equities between the plaintiff's interest in peace and quiet against the interests of the defendant and the public usually although not always is resolved in favor of the latter parties. However, a noise can be such a serious invasion of the rights of an owner or possessor of property as to amount to a taking.

The usual remedy in cases dealing with complaints of excessive noise is an award of money damages against the noisemaker. Injunctive relief may also be sought, especially when the noise is merely annoying, and not causing any injury to person or property. However, such injunctions are rarely granted. Public policy considerations usually outweigh personal interest if the noisemaker can show that he is engaged in a socially useful activity. Noise required to run an airport, for example, will generally be held to be permitted on the ground of public interest.

There have been several attempts by local governments to regulate airplane noise by ordinance. The courts have held that the federal government has preempted the field and that such ordinances are invalid.

V

PESTICIDES

Pesticides embrace a wide variety of chemical compounds for controlling undesirable forms of life which threaten man, his possessions, and portions of the natural environment that he values. A report of the Department of Health, Education and Welfare Secretary's Commission on "Pesticides and Their Relationship to Environmental Health" of December 1969 pointed to some 900 active pesticidal chemicals formulated into over 60,000 preparations in the United States. In 1968, production and sales of synthetic organic pesticides reached 1.2 billion pounds, of which about 20 per cent was exported.

Slightly more than half of all pesticides made are used in farming. About 45 per cent is actually used on crops. Government agencies use about 5 per cent; residential and industrial users account for the rest. At the current growth rate--almost 15 per cent a year--a billion pounds of pesticides will soon be applied annually in this country. Most of the increase over the past few years is laid to the expanded use of herbicides. Insecticides and fungicides have not expanded as much. Pesticides can be grouped as nonpersistent, moderately persistent, persistent, and permanent, based on how long they last in the environment. These lifetimes are critical in predicting and assessing ecological effects.

A pesticide may move through an ecosystem in many ways. Hard pesticides ingested or otherwise borne by the target species will stay in the environment, possibly to be recycled rapidly or concentrated further through the natural action of food chains if the species is eaten. Most of the volume of pesticides do not reach their target at all.

Whether pesticides are introduced into the environment by spraying or by surface application, air usually is the medium through which the chemicals move to their intended and unintended targets. Very few data exist on pesticides in the air, largely because of a lack of adequate monitoring. Their presence and fate are functions of their chemical nature, physical state, method of application, and atmospheric conditions. It is clear that pesticides may be blown long distances on dust particles.

The persistence of pesticides in the air is influenced by gravitational fallout and washout by rain. They build up in the soil to concentrations which may eventually reach man by a number of routes: through water drawn from the soil by consumable crops, through leaching or washing into water supplies, and by his direct contact with the soil. Pesticides linger on, often to injure organisms and crops which grow later in the same soil.

Pesticides enter water chiefly through spraying, runoff from treated areas, or waste discharge by producers. Percolation through soil to ground water and accidental dumping are minor sources. Pesticides can reach humans directly through drinking water, but the concentration in most cases is far below toxic level. There is no evidence at present that long-term consumption of such water is harmful, although the buildup of pesticides in water may eventually prove dangerous.

Initially, low levels of persistent pesticides in air, soil, and water may be concentrated at every step up the food chain. Minute aquatic organisms and scavengers, which screen water and bottom mud having pesticide levels of a few parts per billion, can accumulate levels measured in a few parts per million--a thousand-fold increase. Oysters, for instance, will concentrate DDT 70,000 times higher in their tissues than it is concentrated in surrounding water, but they partially cleanse themselves in water free of DDT. Fish feeding on lower organisms build up concentrations in their visceral fat which may reach several thousand parts per million and levels in their edible flesh of hundreds of parts per million. Larger animals, such as fish-eating gulls, can further concentrate the chemicals. To date, the effects of pesticides have been studied in less than 1 per cent of the animal species present in the United States.

On the Federal level, pesticide regulation is governed by two statutes. The Federal Insecticide, Fungicide and Rodenticide Act (7 USC 135 et. seq.) administered by the Department of Agriculture, makes it unlawful to ship in interstate commerce any economic poison which is not registered under the Act. The Act requires pesticides and other "economic poisons" to carry labels bearing certain information, including any warnings necessary to prevent human injury. A pesticide which fails to comply with the labeling requirement, or which cannot be rendered safe by any labeling, is misbranded, and the Secretary must refuse or cancel its registration as an economic poison approved for shipment in interstate commerce.

A second statute is the Federal Food, Drug and Cosmetic Act, which required the Food and Drug Administration to establish residue tolerances for all pesticide products designed for use on or in human or animal food. Thus the Federal Insecticide, Fungicide, and Rodenticide Act protects interstate commerce; the Food, Drug, and Cosmetic Act protects the nation's health. The Food and Drug Administration must establish the residue tolerance for a particular use before the Department of Agriculture grants the registration. The law provides for seizure and destruction of commodities that contain pesticide residues in excess of established tolerances.

Forty-eight states have laws, patterned on Federal law, which govern the marketing of pesticides. Thirty-nine states also regulate their use. Most of these states require commercial applicators to obtain licenses or permits. Within the past year, a number of states enacted registrations or laws restricting the marketing or use of certain chemicals, particularly DDT.

Pesticides have been the subject of litigation in several important cases. The Environmental Defense Fund petitioned the Food and Drug Administration of the Department of Health, Education and Welfare to set a "zero tolerance level" which would stop the use of DDT on agricultural commodities. The court ordered that petitioners' proposals for zero tolerances be published in the Federal Register and that HEW begin the administrative proceedings necessary to arrange a hearing on the EDF's petition. The court recommended three possible approaches to banning DDT: (1) Set a zero tolerance, but exempt crops treated with DDT before that tolerance was established; (2) announce an immediate, gradual stepwise reduction in permissible residues; or (3) announce a zero tolerance to take effect at some specific date in the future. It also ordered HEW to consider EDF's evidence on DDT as a cancer-producing agent. If that evidence were determined to be sound, HEW would have to explain how any residue could be considered "safe." Administrative proceedings to consider these alternatives are now under way. Environmental Defense

Fund v. Finch. At the same time, these same petitioners requested an order that the Secretary of Agriculture suspend registration for all uses of DDT immediately. The Secretary cancelled four uses, invited comments on the others, and took no action on the suspension request. The court ordered the Department to begin cancellation proceedings within 30 days or to give detailed reasons for refusing to initiate proceedings. The Department chose the latter alternative and argument on the sufficiency of its reasons has been heard, but the decision of the court has not yet been rendered. Environmental Defense Fund v. Hardin.

While the Federal agencies appear to favor continued use of DDT, it is hopeful that with pesticide regulation becoming one of the functions of the recently established Environmental Protection Agency that the environmentalist position on pesticides will prevail.

VI

LAND USE

Misuse of the land is one of the most serious and difficult challenges to environmental quality, because it is the most out-of-hand and irreversible. Air and water pollution are serious, hard to manage problems, too. But they are worked at with standards, with enforcement tools, and by institutions set up for those specific antipollution purposes. Land use is still not guided by any agreed upon standards. It is instead influenced by a welter of sometimes competing, overlapping government institutions and programs, private and public attitudes and biases, and distorted economic incentives.

The 50 states comprise about 2.3 billion acres of land. Of that, 1.9 billion acres lie in the contiguous 48 states. Nearly 58 per cent of the land area is used for crops and livestock. More than 22 per cent is ungrazed forest land. Less than 3 per cent is in urban and transportation uses, although it is increasing. Areas designed primarily for parks, recreation, wildlife refuges, and public installations and facilities account for about 5 per cent. The rest--12 per cent--is mainly desert, swamp, tundra, and other lands presently of limited use by man.

Almost 59 per cent of the land is in private hands. Thirty-four per cent is owned by the Federal Government. Some 94 per cent of all Federal lands lie in the westernmost states--about half in Alaska alone. About 2 per cent of the nation's land is held by the Indians. The rest--about 5 per cent--is State, city, or county owned.

The techniques for preserving private open space are numerous and varied. They range from condemnation or outright purchase by the government, through governmental regulation such as zoning and governmental incentives by way of tax policies, to private donation. None of these strategies can be relied upon exclusively.

The sovereign power of the states in our system of government is termed the "police power." This term covers a wide array

Land Use in the United States

Land Ownership in the United States

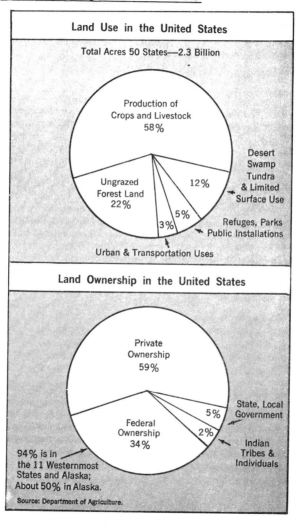

Land Use in the United States

Total Acres 50 States—2.3 Billion

Production of Crops and Livestock 58%

Ungrazed Forest Land 22%

12%

Desert Swamp Tundra & Limited Surface Use

5%

3%

Refuges, Parks Public Installations

Urban & Transportation Uses

Land Ownership in the United States

Private Ownership 59%

Federal Ownership 34%

5%

State, Local Government

2%

Indian Tribes & Individuals

94% is in the 11 Westernmost States and Alaska; About 50% in Alaska.

Source: Department of Agriculture.

Annual Conversion of Rural Land in the United States to Non-Agricultural Uses

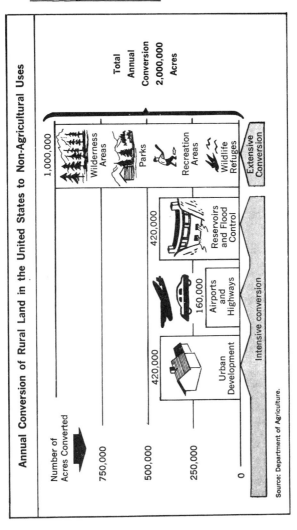

Source: Department of Agriculture.

of land use devices designed to protect the welfare of the general public. Included in the police powers are the power to tax, to condemn land, and to regulate land use. The constitutionality of land use regulation usually turns on any of four questions: (1) Is the regulation reasonably related to a protectable goal? Conservation has been held to be a proper goal of land use regulation. Preservation of aesthetic attributes is another permissible goal for land use regulation, although aesthetic consideration cannot usually serve as the only basis for regulation. Other police power goals--health, safety, welfare, etc.--must usually be involved when regulations designed to protect beauty are proposed. (2) Will similarly situated landowners be treated equally? Effective land regulation requires that different parcels of land be treated differently. But "it is fundamental in zoning policy/ and other land use regulation/ that all property in like circumstances be treated alike." The courts require an over-all plan for land use regulation. Piecemeal regulations ("spot zoning") have been struck down by the courts. (3) Does the regulation deprive the land of substantially all economic value? In the landmark decision in this field, the court said: "An ordinance which permanently so restricts the use of property that it cannot be used for any reasonable purpose, it is plain, beyond regulation, and must be recognized as a taking of the property. The only substantial difference, in such case, between restriction and actual taking, is that restriction leaves the owner subject to the burden of payment of taxation, while outright confiscation would relieve him of that burden." Arverne Bay Construction Company v. Thatcher 278 NY 222, 232, 15 NE2nd 587, 592. (4) Is eminent domain appropriate? As the quote from the previously cited case shows, government may not take rights to land that it ought to pay for under the guise of zoning. It is difficult to predict what the courts will hold as confiscation and regulation. If it is the former, of course, it is an unconstitutional taking and the regulation will be negated.

Zoning is the major police power employed to control land use. It classifies and segregates the land according to the permitted uses. It can curb those uses up to the point of taking private property without compensation. Within each classification, zoning can set limits on the nature, extent and improvement of land. Although it has worked well in well-established communities where there is little land speculation or pressure for new commercial facilities, it has had less success preserving open space or channeling growth in developing areas. While ideally zoning should implement sound land use plans, it does not necessarily do so. It is usually honored in the breach by the granting of variances or amendments once the pressure of development is on.

In many suburbs zoning has become a device to exclude less desirable residential, commercial, and industrial newcomers. In such communities, it is used primarily to discourage the kind of development that will cost more in municipal spending than it will pay in property taxes.

Another method of preserving open space under the police power is subdivision control. Such controls embody some of the most promising tools for regulating urban growth. They comprise all the local ordinances and regulations that tell the landowner what he can and cannot do in dividing his land into lots, and selling them or developing them. Where controls are used solely to benefit the developer economically, they can lead to tedious and unattractive developments with uniform setback and lot size, unimaginative street patterns, and little provision for open space or for commercial facilities within walking distance of homes. On the other hand, when subdivision controls permit cluster development, open space preservation, planned unit development, and other imaginative innovations, they can bring a sense of community and vitality. Subdivision enactments have been upheld as a valid exercise of the police power. But some courts have held that a subdivision enactment is invalid unless it is for a public expense uniquely and specifically attributable to the activity of the developer.

Eminent domain gives to government the right to acquire lands. It may be invoked in the case of a reluctant seller, provided the property is used for the public benefit and there is just compensation. Such acquisition of land by a public authority for open space purposes is the surest method of preserving open spaces. But, unlike land use regulation, it requires public financing. Condemnation for such open space purposes as recreation and flood control have long been recognized by the courts. The crucial element is that the taking must be for a public purpose. Generally, the courts are quite liberal in determining what is a public use. The public use test usually applies to purchase as well as condemnation of open space land.

Tax policy is a vital cog in deciding income and profit for land investors, suburban developers, urban developers, and landlords--the big influencers of land use. Taxation is therefore an essential tool in shaping the man-made environment and preserving the natural environment.

Many states have adopted statutes designed to offer tax incentives to owners who agree to leave their land in open space uses. These statutes offer preferential assessments, guaranteeing that land will be assessed at its open space value, regardless of its development potential, as long as designated open space uses are maintained.

The Federal Public Domain consists of the one third of the land area of the nation owned by the United States government. These public lands are largely in the western states and in Alaska, and many are valuable for minerals, timber, grazing, and recreation.

Management of most Federal natural lands falls under four agencies:

Department of the Interior:	Millions of acres
Bureau of Land Management	470.4
Fish and Wildlife Service	30.5
National Park Service	27.1
Department of Agriculture:	
Forest Service	186.9

Many other forests, parks, and recreation and conservation areas have also been set aside by state and local governments and by citizens' groups with an interest in the natural environment.

The largest part of the public domain is under the jurisdiction of the Bureau of Land Management. Therefore, the best approach to the subject of proper use of public lands is to examine the procedures of this Bureau.

The basic policy question of the general use to which public lands should be put is usually determined by the process of "classification." Classification limits the range of uses to which public lands may be subject. The Classification and Multiple Use Act of 1964 is one of the most important pieces of legislation now governing the public domain. 43 USC #1141 provides, inter alia:

34

Consistent with and supplemental to the Taylor Grazing Act of June 28, 1934, as amended, and pending the implementation of recommendations of the Public Land Law Review Commission:

(a) The Secretary of the Interior shall develop and promulgate regulations containing criteria by which he will determine which of the public lands and other Federal lands, including those situated in the State of Alaska exclusively administered by him through the Bureau of Land Management, shall be (a) disposed of because they are (1) required for the orderly growth and development of a community, or (2) are chiefly valuable for residential, commercial, agricultural (exclusive of lands chiefly valuable for grazing and raising forage crops), industrial, or public uses or development, or (b) retained, at least during this period, in Federal ownership and managed for (1) domestic livestock grazing, (2) fish and wildlife development and utilization, (3) industrial development, (4) mineral production, (5) occupancy, (6) outdoor recreation, (7) timber production, (8) watershed protection, (9) wilderness preservation, or (10) preservation of public values that would be lost if the land passed from Federal ownership . . . .

(b) The Secretary of the Interior shall, as soon as possible, review the public lands as defined herein, in the light of the criteria contained in the regulations issued with this section to determine which lands shall be classified as suitable for disposal and which lands he considers to contain such values as to make them more suitable for retention in Federal ownership for interim management under the principles enunciated in this section. In making his determinations the Secretary shall give due consideration to all pertinent factors, including, but not limited to, ecology, priorities in use, and the relative values of the various resources in particular areas.

43 USC #1413 provides:

> The Secretary of the Interior shall develop and administer for multiple use and sustained yield of the several products and services obtainable therefrom those public lands that are determined to be suitable for interim management in accordance with regulations promulgated pursuant to this sub-chapter.

43 USC #1415 gives the following definitions:

> (a) The term "public lands" means any lands (1) withdrawn or reserved by Executive Order Numbered 6910 of November 26, 1934, as amended, or (2) within a grazing district established pursuant to the Act of June 28, 1934, as amended, or (3) located in the State of Alaska, which are not otherwise withdrawn or reserved for a Federal use or purpose.
>
> (b) "Multiple Use" means the management of the various surface and subsurface resources so that they are utilized in the combination that will best meet the present and future needs of the American people; the most judicious use of land for some or all of these resources or related services over areas large enough to provide sufficient latitude for periodic adjustment in use to conform to changing needs and conditions; the use of some land for less than all of the resources; and harmonious and coordinated management of the various resources, each with the other, without impairment of the productivity of the land, with consideration being given to the relative values of the various resources, and not necessarily the combination of uses that will give the greatest dollar return or the greatest unit output.

(c) "Sustained yield of the several products and services" means the achievement and maintenance of a high-level annual or regular periodic output of the various renewable resources of land without impairment of the productivity of the land.

Public notice is required to be given for all proposed classifications over 2,560 acres. Regulations of the criteria required by 43 USC 1411 were promulgated on October 5, 1965. Classifications are made pursuant to administrative procedures, including hearings, under the criteria regulations. Although the Act is not clear, the Department of the Interior has decided that classifications for retention will continue indefinitely, although the authority to classify expires six months after the Public Land Law Review Commission submits its report. As of January 31, 1969, about 138 million acres were classified for disposal. Another 19 million have been proposed for classification. The Bureau of Land Management has estimated about 10 million acres would be classified for disposal.

The classification decision is of great importance in view of the strong public interest in the manner in which public lands are used generally, and the strong private interest that often exists in the use of particular public lands. Thus if an area of land has been classified for wilderness preservation, economic interests may be effectively barred from exploiting it. But if a conservation group or local citizen wants to object to a proposed use of land by timber, mineral, or other exploitive interests, but the land has already been classified for the use, the conservationists have small basis to object.

Use, retention, and disposal of public lands is governed by numerous statutes. A number of the most important statutes will be described here.

The Taylor Grazing Act of 1934, 43 USC ##315 et. seq., together with the 1934 and 1935 executive withdrawal orders, afford extensive protection for public lands. Under it grazing districts were set and a Grazing Service was established to protect and administer the districts. While the essential purpose of the Act is protection of grazing rights and privileges (which benefits the livestock industry), another purpose is "to provide for the most beneficial use possible of the public range in the interest not only of grazers but also of the public at large." Red Canyon Sheep Co. v. Ickes, 98 F2d 380, 314. This can make it possible to challenge a classification decision by the Secretary of the Interior if, for example, it can be shown that certain land would be more suitable for recreational purposes than for grazing.

Numerous wildlife refuges have been created by Congress, and other refuges have been created by executive order under specified conditions. The President has reserved many refuges on his own initiative. These refuges are administered under the United States Fish and Wildlife Service of the Department of the Interior. Since 1966, they have been administered as the National Wildlife Refuge System. Statutory policy guides for the administration of wildlife refuges are scattered about in Title 16.

The Wilderness Act of 1964 provides congressional protection for several named wilderness areas and provides a plan whereby lands within the National Forests, National Parks and National Wilderness Refuges are to be reviewed so that appropriate areas may be set aside for inclusion in a National Wilderness Preservation System. A wilderness area is defined as "an area where the earth and its community of life are untrammeled by man, where man himself is a visitor who does not remain," 16 USC #1131 (c). It is an area that "has outstanding opportunities for solitude or a primitive and unconfined type of recreation . . . ." 16 USC #1131 (c) (2).

The Secretaries of Agriculture and Interior are required to review all areas within their control to determine whether any should be included in the National Wilderness System. Both Departments are seriously behind in their review of National Parks. Conservation groups have complained that the Federal agencies are not adequately staffed to complete the planning and hearing procedures.

When a party in a public land matter considers an administrative decision unfavorable, judicial review of the decision may be available under the general review provisions of the Administrative Procedure Act, 5 USC ##701-706. None of the public lands statutes provide for judicial review. But there are several procedural obstacles to judicial review as already described in other connections that must be overcome before the courts will deal with the merits of the plaintiff's action. These matters include standing to sue, jurisdictional amount, sovereign immunity, and exhaustion of administrative remedies.

VII

PROCEDURAL ASPECTS OF ENVIRONMENTAL LAW

Standing to Sue

Perhaps the greatest obstacle to overcome in environmental litigation has been how to get into the court in the first place. We will deal here with the issues of procedure in overcoming this frequently fatal obstacle of lack of "standing."

Government is presumed to act in the public interest so that Federal courts are reluctant to allow private citizens to sue public officials on the ground that the public interest has been ignored. When the English common law developed, no mere citizen could sue the king. The doctrine of "sovereign immunity" was gradually refined in this country to allow suits against a public official when he acted beyond his constitutional or statutory authority. In those situations, "the officer is not doing the business which the sovereign has empowered him to do or he is doing it in a way which the sovereign has forbidden."

The United States is immune from suit except when it consents to be sued. Unless the United States has consented to be sued through an Act of Congress, no court in the land has jurisdiction of an action against the United States.

The Federal Administrative Procedures Act first adopted in 1946 defines when a Federal agency subject to its provisions may be sued. But to challenge governmental action the private citizen still has to establish his own standing to bring the suit.

The United States Constitution, Article III, Section 2, provides that courts of the United States shall have jurisdiction only over "cases" or "controversies." If there is no "case" or "controversy" involving the plaintiff, he has no standing.

Traditionally, this has meant that the plaintiff only had standing if he could show that "he has sustained or is immediately in danger of sustaining some direct injury as the result of/ the governmental action/ and not merely that he suffers in some indefinite way in common with people generally."

The plaintiffs in environmental suits are usually conservationist organizations or individuals who suffer no direct personal or economic harm from the project or activity about which they claim. The defendants, therefore, usually raise the defense that the plaintiffs lack standing to sue. But if the suit can be brought in the name of a person who is specially damaged then the "controversy" requirement has been met. This is true no matter how slight the threatened pecuniary loss of that person might be or to what extent that person is merely a plaintiff for a larger group that is paying for the litigation.

In <u>Scenic Hudson Preservation Conference v. Federal Power Commission,</u> a leading case in environmental law, conservationists sought to intervene in an F.P.C. proceeding in which the Consolidated Edison Company of New York had applied for a license to construct a pumped storage hydroelectric project on Storm King Mountain. On appeal the Commission argued that the applicants did not have standing to obtain judicial review because they claimed no economic injury. Responding to this argument, the court said

> Although a "case" or "controversy" which is otherwise lacking cannot be created by statute, a statute may create new interests or rights and thus give standing to one who would otherwise be barred by the lack of a "case" or "controversy." /This requirement of Article III, Section 2/ does not require that an "aggrieved" or "adversely affected" party have a personal economic interest.

But even more significant to the preparation of an environmental case is the court's description of an aggrieved party:

> In order to insure that the Federal Power Commission will adequately protect the public interest in the aesthetic, conservational, and recreational aspects of power development, those who by their activities and conduct have exhibited a special interest in such cases, must be held to be included in the class of "aggrieved" parties under Section 313 (b)/of the Federal Power Act, 16 U.S.C.

> Section 8251 (b)/ . . . . We hold that the Federal
> Power Act gives petitioners a legal right to pro-
> tect their special interests.

The increasing acceptability of the argument that the standing requirement rooted in Article III of the United States Constitution may be satisfied by a showing that (1) the party is "aggrieved" and (2) that his cause has been congressionally recognized within a "relevant" statute, has been demonstrated in subsequent cases.

In Association of Data Processing Serv. Organizations, Inc. v. Camp, the Supreme Court has most recently examined the standing doctrine and announced a new, two-step test for determining "whether the plaintiff alleges that the challenged action has caused him injury in fact, economic or otherwise." If such an injury does not exist, there is a danger that the dispute will not be presented in a truly adversary context. In that case the suit would not be a "case" or "controversy," and thus would be outside the scope of the judicial power as delimited by Article III of the Constitution. If the court is satisfied that the plaintiff has suffered an actual injury, it must ask whether "the interest sought to be protected by the complainant is arguably within the zone of interests to be protected or regulated by the statute or constitutional guarantee in question."

When the Supreme Court agreed to hear this case, conservation groups were concerned that the standing of "public interest plaintiffs" might be inadvertently reduced. The Sierra Club filed an amicus curiae brief with the Supreme Court urging that the Court not use broad language which would have the effect of reducing the standing of public interest plaintiffs in conservation cases. Instead, Mr. Justice Douglas went out of his way by dictum to improve the standing of conservation plaintiffs. In describing the zones of interest to be protected in his second requirement of standing, he states:

> That interest, at times, may reflect 'aesthetic,
> conservational' as well as economic values....
> We mention these noneconomic values to empha-
> size that standing may stem from them as well
> as from the economic injury on which petitioner
> relies here.

41

Every conservation plaintiff can allege and often prove harm to aesthetic, recreational, or conservation values. The harder questions are the last two requirements of the Court, zone of interest and availability of judicial review.

In summary, there is a two-part test for meeting the requirements for standing in environmental cases. First, the plaintiff must show he is "aggrieved" by the action, which can be shown by a long and active interest in environmental activities. Second, a "relevant statute" enunciating Congressional recognition of the environmentalists' cause must be found. This is not a difficult problem; many conservationist statutes contain broad language emphasizing various conservationist goals. Note the following examples:

16 USC #1

(National Park Service must "conserve the scenery and the natural and historic objects and the wild life" in national parks and "provide for the enjoyment of the same in such a manner and by such means as will leave them unimpaired for the enjoyment of future generations");

16 USC #661

("recognizing the vital contribution of our wildlife resources to the Nation, the increasing public interest and significance thereof due to expansion of our national economy and other factors");

16 USC #668aa(a)-(b)

("to provide a program for the conservation, protection, restoration, and propagation of selected species of native fish and wildlife, including migratory birds, that are threatened with extinction," and to "seek to protect species of native fish and wildlife, including migratory birds, that are threatened with extinction, and, insofar as is practicable and consistent with the primary purposes of such bureaus, agencies, and services, shall preserve the habitats of such threatened species on lands under their jurisdiction");

16 USC 695K

("to preserve intact the necessary existing habitat for migratory waterfowl in this vital area of the Pacific flyway, and to prevent depredations of migratory waterfowl on agricultural crops in the Pacific Coast States");

16 USC #1131(a)

("In order to assure that an increasing population, accompanied by expanding settlement and growing mechanization, does not occupy and modify all areas within the United States and its possessions, leaving no lands designated for preservation and protection in their natural condition, it is hereby declared to be the policy of the Congress to secure for the American people of present and future generations the benefits of an enduring resource of wilderness.")

16 USC #1271

("that certain selected rivers of the nation which, with their immediate environments, possess outstandingly remarkable scenic, recreational, geological, fish and wildlife, historic, cultural, or other similar values, shall be preserved in free-flowing condition, and that they and their immediate environments shall be protected for the benefit and enjoyment of present and future generations. The Congress declares that the established national policy of dam and other construction at appropriate sections of the rivers of the United States needs to be complemented by a policy that would preserve other selected rivers or sections

43

thereof in their free-flowing condition to protect
the water quality of such rivers and to fulfil other
vital national conservation purposes. ")

Furthermore, the broad policy declarations of the National
Environmental Policy Act puts the Congressional seal of approval
on virtually all conservationist activity. While there has been a
large number of cases upholding the standing of conservationist
organizations, a Federal court in Sierra Club v. Hickel in September, 1970, held that the Sierra Club had no standing to con-
test the allegedly improper granting of a permit to Walt Disney
Enterprises to build the Mineral King Ski Resort in the Sequoia
National Game Refuge. The result of the pending appeal to the
Supreme Court may be a definitive statement on conservationists'
standing to protect the environment.

Pleadings and Theories of Action

Another fundamental problem for environmental lawyers is
finding a substantive theory to support environmental litigation.
The availability of administrative remedies in the area of pollution does not preclude an action at law or suit in equity for injuries
to private rights caused by pollution.

A person whose property or personal enjoyment thereof
is affected by a private nuisance may sue to have the activity enjoined. A person may sue to enjoin a public nuisance if he suffers
some special damage from it. A private nuisance is defined and
distinguished from a trespass:

> Trespass and private nuisance are separate fields
> of tort liability relating to actionable interference
> with the possession of land. They may be dis-
> tinguished by comparing the interest invaded; an
> actionable invasion of a possessor's interest in
> the exclusive possession of land is a trespass; an
> actionable invasion of a possessor's interest in
> the use and enjoyment of his land is a nuisance.

Whether or not a particular annoyance or inconvenience (or pollution) is sufficient to constitute a nuisance depends on its effect

44

upon an ordinary reasonable man. This means, essentially, that the court will consider the equities between the parties. Also, the court will consider the availability of an adequate remedy at law as well as the nature, extent, and irreparable character of the injury or wrong sought to be remedied.

We have considered a general distinction between a nuisance and a trespass. A more definitive consideration of what constitutes a trespass is:

> "...any intrusion which invades the possessor's protected interest in exclusive possession, whether that intrusion is by visible or invisible pieces of matter or by energy which can be measured only by the mathematical language of the physicist."

This broad definition shows that the polluter may trespass upon one's property by causing invisible particulates, gas or even noise, to invade the possessor's land.

The same general considerations relative to balancing the equities between the parties in granting of an injunction for nuisance apply with respect to the granting of an injunction for the defendant's continuing trespass. The factors that the court will consider in this situation are clarity of proof, character of the area, nature of the industry, priority of occupation of the respective parcels of land. It should be noted, moreover, that the aggrieved party may attack the polluter on additional grounds by citing a violation of a pollution statute or even a zoning ordinance as a basis for his suit to enjoin.

The party seeking injunctive relief from the polluter should generally proceed, if possible, under a theory of trespass, rather than nuisance. The reason for this is that an invasion will be easy to prove under the broader definition discussed above, and there is no bar from recovery just because the plaintiff may be supersensitive.

Defenses to nuisance and trespass actions include prescriptive rights and statutory authorization. If a private nuisance has continued for a period in excess of the applicable statute of limitations, a prescriptive right is created. Frequently statutes provide that nothing which is done or maintained under the express authority

45

of a statute can be deemed a nuisance. But such statutes do not provide a defense if there was negligence or if the specific act creating the nuisance was not expressly authorized.

A third approach is a negligence action. While there is the advantage that such an action offers the greater likelihood that punitive damages will be awarded, the disadvantages are more difficult to overcome because of the difficulty in proving causation and the problem of standard of care.

Statutory causes of action are for the most part very new and it is not possible at this point of time to predict whether they will prove to be significant. Michigan's Environmental Protection Act of 1970 is the nation's first such statute. It allows citizens to bring suits "for the protection of the air, water and other natural resources and the public trust therein from pollution, impairment or destruction." Section 3 of that Act states that the plaintiff has made a prima facie case when he shows the defendant has polluted or is likely to pollute the air, water, etc. It is then up to the defendant to rebut. The defendant may show, as an affirmative defense, that there is no feasible alternative to his conduct or that his conduct is "consistent with the promotion of the public health, safety and welfare in light of the state's paramount concern for the protection of its natural resources from pollution, impairment or destruction." Other bills, similar to the Michigan act, are now being considered by a half dozen states.

A second statutory cause of action is provided in Section 12 of the Clean Air Amendments of 1970 which allows citizens to enforce emission standards and orders related thereto and other duties under the Air Quality Act. It has been suggested by numerous authorities that there is a cause of action in Section 101 (c) of the National Environmental Policy Act which states:

> The Congress recognizes that each person should enjoy a healthful environment and that each person has a responsibility to contribute to the preservation and enhancement of the environment.

A final possibility is the qui tam action under the Refuse Act, whereby the citizen sues to collect the penalty provided by that statute.

The third category of suits is by private citizens against Federal officers or agencies to protect some environmental value. This has become the most prominent type of recent suit in environmental litigation because the common law cause of action has not been adequate and the statutory causes of action are very new. Furthermore, the government has been slower than the citizen groups to attack environmental problems.

The first required element in such suits is that a Federal contact or action must be involved. This can mean a Federal project, such as the Cross Florida Barge Canal. Or it may simply involve a Federal grant of money or a Federal permit. Second, the Federal action in question must be in conflict with a statute designed to protect the environmental value in question. Examples of such statutes are the Federal Insecticide, Fungicide, and Rodenticide Act, 7 USC Sec. 135 et. seq., the Wilderness Act, 16 USC #1131 et. seq., the Air Quality Act, 42 USC, et. al. The most important act is the National Environmental Policy Act, which covers most Federal actions. In short, a Federal officer must take unlawful action or fail to take lawful action. Third, the plaintiff must have standing to sue. The discussion in the first section of this chapter deals with this issue. Fourth, the court must have jurisdiction to review the action of the government official. Fifth, the administrative remedies must have been exhausted. Sixth, the problem must be suitable for equitable relief. And seventh, the case must be strong on the merits as the presumption is that the administrator is acting properly.

Injunctions

Most environmental law suits seek injunctive relief, usually to stop a public agency from approving a project or to order a private person or a public authority to stop work on one. Actions for damages are impractical since there is no way to determine the public's loss from environmental deterioration. But seeking injunctive relief imposes several difficult burdens on conservationists.

Injunctions are an extraordinary remedy which courts grant sparingly. Generally, the plaintiff must demonstrate that he will suffer irreparable injury and that no other adequate remedy is available. "Balancing the equities" is the measure by which courts render their decisions in actions seeking injunctive relief. Generally speaking, the economic effects of the injunction at least at this stage of environmental law still persuades the courts more than the effects on the environment.

The Class Action

The class action is one of the most effective ways to move against polluters. This procedure makes it possible for the victims of pollution to bargain effectively with polluters. It also makes it feasible to assert claims for damages that would otherwise be too small to warrant the expense of a lawsuit. Individual plaintiffs must meet the jurisdictional amount of $10,000 required in Federal cases.

The Supreme Court recently dealt a serious blow to the possibility of using the class action as a general antipollution procedural device in the Federal Courts. Since the pecuniary damages suffered by any single pollution victim rarely totals $10,000, environmental class actions against non-governmental defendants in Federal courts are foreclosed.

A bill specifically authorizing environmental class actions was introduced in the last session of Congress and it is probable that sooner or later such legislation will be passed. While a number of state statutes make class actions possible restrictive interpretations of those statutes by the courts diminish the potential success of using such statutes for this purpose.

Burden of Proof

The assignment of the burden of proof may be a crucial factor in determining the outcome in environmental litigation. Those seeking to establish environmental quality are usually plaintiffs in lawsuits and thus have the burden of proving basic issues. The courts, however, have frequently lowered the burden of proof requirements on plaintiffs when they are persuaded that the merits of the case are in their favor. Nevertheless, present procedures generally favor the defendant and environmentalists would probably be wise to seek to change burden of proof rules and procedures.

Constitutional Aspects

It has been argued that the "right to a decent environment" is a constitutional protection provided in the 9th Amendment of the United States Constitution.

> The enumeration in the Constitution, of certain rights, shall not be construed to deny or disparage others retained by the people.

This Amendment made certain that the Bill of Rights could not be interpreted as a limitation of other rights not specified. The source of interest in the 9th Amendment came from a Supreme Court case, Griswold v. Connecticut, wherein the Court invalidated a Connecticut anti-birth control statute as incompatible with a constitutionally protected right of privacy. Mr. Justice Douglas' majority opinion, which was based on the notion that "specific guarantees in the Bill of Rights have penumbras, formed by emanations from those guarantees that help give them life and substance, "referred briefly to the 9th Amendment. The concurring opinion of Mr. Justice Goldberg, in which Chief Justice Warren and Mr. Justice Brennan joined, relied heavily on the 9th Amendment as proof of the existence of "basic and fundamental rights which the Constitution guaranteed to the people" beyond those enumerated in the first eight Amendments.

Conservationists have argued that the prohibition in the Fifth and 14th Amendments against uncompensated taking is a constitutional protection against environmental destruction. There is a bill to amend the Constitution to provide specifically for a right of environmental quality. But as Professor Joseph Sax, the leading environmental lawyer, has pointed out, while "some say that a constitutional amendment 'could do for the environment what the Fifth Amendment has done for civil rights, ' a slight emendation of this statement is required for accuracy's sake--it is what the Constitution and the courts have done that we recall with pride. "

A number of state constitutions have adopted specific grants of environmental rights. The New York Constitution, Article XIV, states:

The policy of the state shall be to conserve and protect its natural resources and scenic beauty and encourage the development and improvement of its agricultural lands for the production of food and other agricultural products . . . .

The Public Trust Doctrine

A judicially created doctrine has emerged in recent years which has been advocated as a most effective weapon in achieving legal control over environmental quality. This is the public trust doctrine. An elaborate account of the development of this doctrine is contained in a long article by Professor Sax, "The Public Trust Doctrine in Natural Resource Law: Effective Judicial Intervention, " 68 Michigan Law Review 471 (1970). Sax traces the origin and development of the idea that certain public resources, such as shorelines, rivers, seas, and other large bodies of water, are held by the government in trust for the people and that there are definite limitations on the power of the government to dispose of these resources. He argues that it should be equally applicable to other types of controversies, such as those concerning air pollution, pesticides, rights of way for utilities, and in some cases wetland filling on private lands. This article has been much cited by the courts and by writers on environmental law to such a degree that it deserves the attention of all those interested in the development of environmental law.

VIII

THE INTERNATIONAL ROLE IN ENVIRONMENTAL QUALITY

It should be obvious that environmental problems do not stop at national boundaries nor are they stopped by ideological barriers. Air and water pollution are environmental problems that have international implications. The smokestacks of one country can pollute the air of another. Toxic effluents poured into an international river can kill fish in a neighboring nation and ultimately pollute international waterways. Even in Antarctica, thousands of miles from pollution sources, evidence of DDT and lead have appeared on that "white continent." No longer can we speak of anything being "as pure as the driven snow."

But air and water pollution are not the only environmental problems that have international aspects. Some world resources such as seabed minerals and ocean fish can be effectively dealt with only by international agreement. What nations do to clean up domestic pollution affects international commerce since the costs of pollution control can change the competitive position of a nation's business internationally just as it has shown to be the case domestically. And how nations regulate international transportation and imports to eliminate sources of pollution can also have a profound impace on trade. Nations can achieve economies and foreign policy benefits by undertaking joint research and environmental information sharing with other nations.

The National Environmental Policy Act directed all agencies of the United States Federal government to recognize the worldwide and long-range character of environmental problems. Where consistent with American foreign policy, it directs the agencies to support initiatives, resolutions, and programs designed to maximize international cooperation and prevent a decline in the quality of mankind's environment.

The United States is engaged in international cooperation on environmental matters through a number of varied channels. These include the United Nations and its specialized agencies and

51

other intergovernmental organizations such as NATO, the Economic Commission for Europe and the Organization for Economic Cooperation and Development. It works with nongovernment organizations such as the International Biological Program and the International Union for the Conservation of Nature and Natural Resources.

The United Nations

Economic Commission for Europe. The ECE, one of the four regional U.N. commissions on economic and social matters, is composed of the European members of the United Nations and the United States. Its current activities include air and water pollution control, urban development, and exchanges regarding government policy problems in these fields. This agency will assume the main responsibility for a U.N. Conference on Environment to be held in 1972. The ECE is important as a forum for international environmental cooperation because it includes most of the major industrialized countries of the world, East and West, in working-level discussions of environmental problems.

Intergovernmental Maritime Consultative Organization. Since its creation in 1959, IMCO has encouraged an exchange of research and information on the rapid, safe, and workable handling of oil spills and other aspects of ocean pollution. It has established an international mechanism for reporting oil spills. In 1969 IMCO convened major international legal conferences on marine pollution. One proposed strengthening the 1954 Treaty on Prevention of Pollution of the Sea by Oil. The other proposed two new conventions to permit action to deal with damaged vessels threatening oil spills on the high seas and to fix liability for the costs of oil spill cleanup. These treaties have been ratified by the U.S. Senate.

U.N. Educational, Scientific and Cultural Organization. UNESCO promotes scientific investigation of man-induced changes in the character of the oceans. It supports programs to identify effects of waste disposal at sea and to prevent depletion or extinction of valuable marine species because of man's activities. UNESCO-sponsored studies of atmospheric pollution are presently underway. In 1968, UNESCO convened the International Conference on the Rational Use and Conservation of Resources of the Biosphere. Out of recommendations of that conference, it is developing a long-term, comprehensive program of research and action on environmental problems, called Man and the Biosphere.

World Health Organization. WHO has conducted studies of coastal pollution and lends technical guidance on coastal water quality and on ways to prevent pollution. It is developing a worldwide program of monitoring certain environmental conditions which directly affect health. WHO has also assisted many member countries in carrying out field projects on waste disposal and water pollution control.

Food and Agriculture Organization. FAO undertakes studies on water quality criteria for fish, on pesticides and pollution, on pulp and paper mill effluents, and on sewage effluents. Although more concerned with pollution of inland waters, FAO has also turned to the study, monitoring, and management of the sources and effects of pollution on ocean fisheries. FAO also carries out ecological studies and surveys connected with land use, stressing increased productivity and management of natural resources, particularly in the developing countries. FAO has programs in wildlife management, in tourist development and protein production, in national park development, and in the traditional agricultural and forestry areas.

World Meteorological Organization. WMO has launched the World Weather Watch to improve the collection of meteorological data for forecasting and for studies of atmospheric pollutants. Basic research is being promoted and coordinated through the Global Atmospheric Research Program jointly organized by WMO and the International Council of Scientific Unions. Studies of the meteorological factors involved in air pollution are being conducted by two WMO commissions.

International Atomic Energy Agency. IAEA environmental activities concentrate on pollution from radioactive substances. It draws up regulations, conducts programs for exchanging information, and supports research projects. IAEA has published guidebooks on nuclear safety and radioactive waste management.

With WHO and UNESCO, it has set up a worldwide sampling network to measure the amount of radioactivity in precipitation and is working on techniques for measuring atmospheric and other environmental radioactivity.

Other Intergovernmental Bodies

NATO Committee on Challenges of Modern Society (CCMS). This committee is designed to consider specific problems of the human environment. It has underway eight pilot studies, and in five of them two or more of the member countries collaborate. The studies are on (1) disaster assistance (United States and Italy), (2) air pollution (United States, Turkey, and Germany), (3) road safety (United States and Germany), (4) open-water pollution (Belgium, Portugal, Canada, and France), (5) inland water pollution (Canada, France, United States, and Belgium), (6) scientific knowledge and decision-making (Germany), (7) motivation in a modern industrial society (United Kingdom), and (8) environment in the strategy of regional development (France).

Organization for Economic Cooperation and Development. The OECD, an assembly of the industrialized nations of Western Europe and North America, with Japan, has active programs on water resources management, air pollution, and pesticides.

Organization of African Unity. The OAU has directed attention to environmental problems and planning through the African Convention on the Conservation of Nature and Natural Resources, signed by representatives of 38 African nations at the OAU Summit Meeting in 1968. This convention, developed on the request of the OAU by the IUCN, with cooperation by FAO and UNESCO, is based on broad ecological principles and covers management, utilization, and preservation of natural resources including soil, water, vegetation and fauna, and also includes aspects of research, education, administration, and legislation.

Organization of American States. Through the OAS the Latin American Convention on Nature Protection and Wildlife Preservation in the Western Hemisphere was prepared in 1940, and subsequently ratified by the United States and 9 other American nations.

The OAS has recently updated the Convention annex lists of threatened species, and is developing appropriate research programs which bear on the articles of convention.

Council of Europe. This assemblage of European nations is making a commitment to environmental quality through its development of the European Conservation Year, initiated in January 1970. Each participating nation has developed its own major conservation program, and the Council serves as a point of liaison and coordination. The programs range from public education in pollution control to programs of basic ecological research.

Bilateral Cooperation

The United States is cooperating bilaterally with Japan, Germany, France, the Soviet Union, and Canada in joint research and information sharing.

With Japan the United States has arrangements for the exchange of scientific and technological information on air pollution, water pollution, toxic microorganisms, wind and seismic damage, and undersea technology. The United States-German program concerns coal dust, water pollution, air pollution control, urban planning, and noise abatement. The United States-Soviet Exchange Agreement covers oceanography, urban transportation, air and water pollution, and other environmental problems.

Cooperation between the United States and Canada on environmental problems has a long history. Their joint attention is now focused on the Great Lakes, St. Lawrence River water boundary, and on the Arctic region. United States-Canada agreements on the Great Lakes go back to the Boundary Waters Treaty of 1906. The Great Lakes is the largest fresh water body in the world. Most of the population of Canada and much of that of the United States lives near its borders, and pollution of the Great Lakes concerns both nations. The intergovernmental body chiefly responsible is the International Joint Commission of the United States and Canada.

The Arctic region, a "last frontier" of natural resources in the Northern Hemisphere, is an area of growing importance in U.S.-Canadian consideration of environmental problems. Bordering international waters, it is important to the development of the United States and the North American continent in part because it affords the shortest distance between Eurasia and North America and in part because of its mineral resources.

The Arctic Ocean makes the United States a neighbor to five nations--the U.S.S.R., Norway, Denmark, Canada, and Iceland. Still other nations share concern over exploration, settlement, and exploitation of the Arctic region. Environmental quality there is a new opportunity for cooperation among all these nations.

Nongovernmental Organizations

The International Council of Scientific Unions initiated the International Biological Program, a nongovernmental international scientific research project covering the biological aspects of the world's physical environment. The 5-year action program started in 1967 now involves scientists from more than 60 countries.

The International Union for Conservation of Nature and Natural Resources (IUCN) was founded in 1948. It comprises 29 nations and several hundred nonpolitical organizations from about 80 countries and maintains headquarters in Morges, Switzerland. The Union seeks to initiate and promote scientifically based action to preserve the natural environment, life forms, and resources. It works through commissions on ecology, species survival, national parks, education, and environmental policy and administration. The IUCN has consultative status with the United Nations and various regional international groups.

ANALYSIS OF
ANTI-POLLUTION LEGISLATION AND CASE LAW

I. Federal Legislation
II. Representative State Legislation
III. Excerpts from Leading Cases

I

SUMMARY OF FEDERAL LEGISLATION

Air Quality Act of 1967 (AIR)

The Department of Health, Education, and Welfare is authorized to designate air quality control regions for the purpose of establishing ambient air quality standards. The Act urges states to set up air quality standards and plans for enforcement of standards based on air quality criteria issued by HEW. However, the Act does not prevent the adoption of higher air quality standards than the HEW criteria. If a state fails to establish standards, HEW may promulgate them for the state. And once standards have been established, if a state fails to take reasonable action to enforce them, the U. S. Attorney General may take abatement action if the pollution originating in that state affects persons in another state. If it affects only citizens in the state of origin, the Attorney General may take action even if standards have not yet been established. The National Air Pollution Control Administration (NAPCA) is the division of HEW that is responsible for administration of the Act.

Airport and Airway Development Act (NOISE)

Declares that airport development projects shall provide for the protection of the environment. The Secretary of Transportation is required to consult with the Secretaries of the Interior, Agriculture, and Health, Education, and Welfare, and the National Council on Environmental Quality before approving projects for new or expanded air transport facilities. Such consultation by the Secretaries and the Council must consider the potential harm to the environment represented by the project. One of the most vital threats to consider is excessive noise of aircraft and its effect on fish and wildlife, use of recreational facilities, and general peace and tranquility. There is a further requirement in the Act that opportunity for public hearings to consider "environmental effects" be afforded prior to approval of a project.

The Anadromous Fish Act of 1965

Authorizes federal-state cooperation for the conservation, development, and enhancement of anadromous fish (which as part of their life cycle must swim down certain streams to the ocean and later ascend these same streams to spawn) resources and to prevent their depletion from various sources, including water resources development such as a hydroelectric project dam. However, the adverse effects on such fish must be balanced against the advantages that accrue from dams and the water they store, viz., maintenance of constant river flow, flood control, a source of needed power, and new recreation facilities.

Classification and Multiple Use Act of 1964

"Classification" is the process by which the basic policy question of the general use to which public lands should be put is determined. Such classification limits the range of uses to which public lands may be subject. Under this Act, the Secretary of Interior has the responsibility of classifying all public lands administered by him through the Bureau of Land Management. He must determine first which lands should be disposed of by the Federal government and which should be retained and managed, and second, to what use those lands should be put.

The Delaware River Basin Compact (WATER)

A Commission, known as the Delaware River Basin Commission, represented by the governors of four basin states (New York, New Jersey, Pennsylvania, and Delaware) and the Federal government, is empowered to formulate a plan for developing the basin's water resources, and may adopt provisions to control and abate water pollution enforceable by the courts. The Commission also has broad authority to allocate river water and to build dams and reservoirs, and may construct sewage treatment plants and levy user fees.

Department of Transportation Act of 1966 (LAND USE)

The policy enunciated by this (and the Federal Highway Act of 1966) is that publicly owned lands of scenic, historic, or recreational significance shall be protected from the threat of inadequately planned highway projects. Therefore, the Secretary of Transportation must give full consideration to the protection of environmental resources before he can approve Federal-aid highway projects. When applying for Federal assistance for a highway program, a state must certify to the Secretary that it has held public hearings or has afforded the opportunity for such hearings. The state must also consider the impact on the environment of the proposed construction.

Federal Food, Drug, and Cosmetic Act (PESTICIDES)

Pesticide regulation is governed by this statute. It prevents the use of pesticides found to be unsafe by experts on raw agricultural commodities unless they are within "tolerance levels" set up by the Secretary of Health, Education, and Welfare, or are specifically exempted. The Secretary may set a zero tolerance level if justified. Interested parties may request a repeal of the tolerance for any commodity.

Federal Insecticide, Fungicide, and Rodenticide Act (PESTICIDES)

This Act precludes the sale of pesticides in interstate commerce unless they have been registered with a division of the Department of Agriculture. Pesticides may not be registered unless they are properly labelled. A label is not considered proper if no directions for safe application of a pesticide can be written. The Department of Agriculture can cancel the pesticide's registration if it does not comply with the requirements of the statute. But the pesticide may continue on the market during the process of hearings before an advisory committee and a later public hearing. However, the Department may suspend registration of a pesticide immediately in cases of "imminent hazard to the public."

The Federal Water Pollution Control Act (WATER)

This is the basic statute covering Federal water pollution control activities. It establishes two policies. (1) "To enhance the quality and value of our water resources and to establish a national policy for the prevention, control, and abatement of water pollution." (2) "To recognize, preserve, and protect the primary responsibilities and rights of the States in preventing and controlling water pollution . . . ." The agency responsible for administering and enforcing the provisions of the Act is the Federal Water Pollution Administration. The Act sets forth the procedures for the adoption of water quality standards by the states.

Fish and Wildlife Coordination Act (WILDLIFE)

This Act provides that "wildlife conservation shall receive equal consideration and be coordinated with other features of water-resources programs" and that government agencies must "consult with the United States Fish and Wildlife Service . . . with a view to the conservation of wildlife resources by preventing loss of and damage to such resources . . . ."

National Environmental Policy Act (GENERAL)

This Act declares environmental quality to be a national policy and instructs all Federal agencies and departments to make a bona fide examination of ecological and environmental factors before making any decision that might affect the environment. Nearly every project of important environmental value is assisted by Federal funding or must receive some Federal approval. The courts are empowered to interpret Federal policies, regulations, and statutes in accordance with the policies of the Act. All Federal agencies are instructed to include a "detailed statement by the responsible official" on five environmental factors in every recommendation or report on proposed legislation.

Refuse Act of 1899 (WATER)

While this Act has been in existence as long as it has the great increase in water pollution since its enactment demonstrates the consequences of negligence in enforcement. The Act provides:

"It shall not be lawful to throw, discharge, or deposit, or cause, suffer, or procure to be thrown, discharged, or deposited either from or out of any ship, barge, or other floating craft of any kind, or from the shore, wharf, manufacturing establishment, or mill of any kind, any refuse matter of any kind or description whatever other than the flowing from streets and sewers and passing therefrom in a liquid state, into any navigable water of the United States, or into any tributary of any navigable water from which the same shall float or be washed into such navigable water; and it shall not be lawful to deposit, or cause, suffer, or procure to be deposited material of any kind in any place on the bank of any navigable water, or on the bank of any tributary of any navigable water, either by ordinary or high tides, or by storms or floods, or otherwise, whereby navigation shall or may be impeded or obstructed: Provided, That nothing herein contained shall extend to, apply to, or prohibit the operations in connection with the improvement of navigable waters or construction of public works, considered necessary and proper by the United States officers supervising such improvement or public work: And provided further, That the Secretary of the Army, whenever in the judgment of the Chief of Engineers anchorage and navigation will not be injured thereby, may permit the deposit of any material above mentioned in navigable waters, within limits to be defined and under conditions to be prescribed by him, provided application is made to him prior to depositing such material; and whenever any permit is so granted the conditions thereof shall be strictly complied with, and any violation thereof shall be unlawful."

Rivers and Harbors Act of 1899 (WATER)

Section 17 of this Act instructs the Justice Department to enforce the Refuse Act. It prohibits the obstruction of a navigable waterway without the consent of the Corps of Engineers. This Act provides for stiff penalties for polluters ranging from a minimum fine of $500 to a maximum of $2500, or by imprisonment for not less than 30 days nor more than one year, or by both such fine and imprisonment, in the discretion of the court. The statute also provides for a "bounty" by offering one-half of fines collected to the person or persons giving information which leads to conviction.

II

SUMMARY OF SELECTED STATE
WATER POLLUTION CONTROL STATUTES

New York

The Department of Environmental Conservation (DEC) with approval of the State Environmental Board (SEB), consisting of 15 members, is the body which formulates water pollution standards. Ch. 140, Art. 4 #100 (1970). This Board may hold hearings and subpoena witnesses and documents. Ch. 140, Art. 2 #15 (8). It may investigate sources of pollution by entering private property at reasonable times. Ch. 140, Art. 2, #15(7). The Board may order a polluter to abate pollution after a public hearing, Pub. H.L. #1223(2), and it can issue permits for waste discharge. Pub. H.L. #1230(1).

The Attorney General is the enforcing officer for water pollution standards. Ch. 111, 1/2 ##1042, 1046. He may bring suit for injunction or penalty in municipal or county court. Pub. H.L. ##1250, 1251, 1252. Violations carry $250-2400 fine plus $500 for each day of violation. Willful violation carries $250-2500 fine and/or one year imprisonment. Pub. H.L. #1250, 1252.

In an emergency situation the Public Health Commissioner may order immediate abatement of any condition or activity, without prior hearing, when such condition or activity constitutes a danger to the health of the public. Pub. H.L. #16. The Department of Environmental Conservation (DEC) may order an immediate abatement of a dangerous situation. Ch. 140, Art. 2, #16. DEC may amend, adopt, or repeal any standards, rules, or regulations required to carry out the purpose of the Act, except that basic environmental quality standards need the approval of the State Environmental Board (SEB).

The public has a right of action by bringing its complaint to DEC. Ch. 140, Art. 2, #14.4d. The alleged polluter's appeal rights are provided for by making all orders and determinations of DEC reviewable by competent courts. Pub. H.L. #1244.

Wisconsin

The body formulating water pollution standards is the Department of Natural Resources (DNR). Seven members are appointed by the Governor with the advice and consent of the Senate. #144.023 (1)(b). The powers of this body include creation of long range water resources plans. #144.025(2)(a). It sets rules for construction and operation of water pollution prevention and after hearing systems. #144.025(2)(c). The Department issues orders to comply with pollution laws, including installation of new treatment plants. #144.025(2)(d)(1)(r). It approves all large well construction and operation. #144.025(2)(e). It investigates and inspects private property for compliance with orders. #144.025(2)(f). The agency can enter into agreements with other states with approval of the Governor. #144.025(2)(j). It may take the action directed and charge the owners costs. #144.025(2)(s). The DNR may require report by industrial discharger of any waste. #144.555.

The Attorney General enforces water pollution standards in the state. A suit for injunction in circuit court of county where pollution occurred is the enforcement procedure. #144.536. Violation of sewage regulation by a municipality carries a fine of $100-500 per day. #144.05.

In an emergency situation, when the public health is endangered, DNR may issue temporary emergency orders; but a public hearing will follow as soon as possible after the order. #144.025 (2)(d).

Six or more citizens may force a public hearing by a verified complaint to DNR. #144.537. But a malicious or bad faith complaint by citizens is recoverable in civil action. #144.537. In any case, alleged polluters may ask DNR for a review of its orders. #144.56(1). All such orders are subject to review by a competent court. #144.56(2).

SUMMARY OF SELECTED STATE
AIR POLLUTION CONTROL STATUTES

Michigan

The agency which sets standards is a nine-member commission within the Department of Health, consisting of three public officials and six appointed private citizens. #336.13. A vote of six is required to effect any rule. #336.17.

The Commission, through the Department of Health, is authorized to bring any action if violators do not comply with abatement directives. #336.28. The Commissioner of Health is the enforcement officer of the Commission. #336.16.

The Commission's powers include: (1) Inspections (#336.26), (2) Abatement orders (#336.22(3)), and (3) Injunction or other legal procedures (#336.28). The penalty is a fine of $500 plus $100 per day. #336.26.

There are no emergency provisions.

Public action may be taken by an action for declaratory or equitable relief. Act 127, Public Acts of 1970.

Pennsylvania

The standard setting body is the Air Pollution Commission within the Department of Health. There are eleven members. Five government officers and six private citizens are appointed to the Commission. #4002(a), 4005(d)(2).

The enforcement agency is the Department of Health. Its powers are (1) Inspection (#4004(1)), (2) Abatement orders (#4004 (4.1)), (3) Fines of $100-500 (#4009(a)), (4) Misdemeanor charge can be brought on second offense (#4009(b)).

There are no emergency provisions and no public right of action.

ANALYSIS OF THE
ARIZONA AIR POLLUTION CONTROL LAWS

Arizona's air pollution control laws are aimed at that state's sources of pollution. These include copper smelters and coal-fired electric power plants. In its declaration of policy, the legislature stated that "no further degradation of air in the state of Arizona by any industrial polluters shall be tolerated."

The statute gives state health officials original jurisdiction and control over any air pollution source capable of generating 75 tons or more of pollutants a day. The state also has original jurisdiction over motor vehicles, combustion engines, and machinery which are operated in more than one county.

The State will control any polluting activities of its own agencies or political subdivisions, such as cities and counties.

Other air pollution sources remain under the jurisdiction of county health authorities. The Board of Health may assume control over any of these remaining sources.

The law creates a permit system requiring that anyone who installs or operates equipment which may cause air pollution must first obtain a state or county permit. Before permits are issued, however, the equipment must be inspected and tested.

Polluters whose machinery cannot meet control regulations set by the Board of Health may obtain conditional permits. These conditional permits allow the polluters additional time for compliance, but also require that he submit a detailed plan for complying with regulations.

Conditional permits granted by the state are limited to one year, but may be renewed by the State Air Pollution Control Hearing Board. The maximum time permitted for the original permit and any extension is three years.

Construction of air pollution control equipment must be initiated in the first year of the conditional permit, and must be completed within three years. Renewals of the conditional permits are granted only if the polluters have abided by the terms of the permit.

If at the end of three years the polluter has not complied because of conditions beyond his control, the Board may grant him one more year in which to comply.

III

EXCERPTS FROM LEADING CASES
ON ENVIRONMENTAL LAW

U.S. v. Bishop Processing Company, 287 F Supp 624 (1968)
Thomsen, C.J.,

This action has been brought by the United States under the Clean
Air Act (the Act), ... The government seeks to enjoin Bishop
Processing Company (the defendant), the operator of a rendering
and animal reduction plant near Bishop, Worcester County, Maryland, from discharging malodorous air pollutants, which it is alleged, move across the state line and pollute the air in and around
Selbyville, Delaware. Defendant has filed a motion to dismiss
the complaint on four grounds, namely: (I) that the Act is an unconstitutional attempt by Congress to control purely local intrastate activities over which Congress has no power to legislate;
(II) that the complaint fails to state a cause of action under the
Act; (III) that the requisite administrative steps have not been
adequately defined or properly concluded as required by law; and
(IV) that remedial action concerning defendant's alleged pollution
was and is currently pending in a state court in Maryland, and that
this Court cannot take jurisdiction under the Act while such an action is pending.

. . . .

The movement of pollutants across a state line is a proper
jurisdictional basis for the provisions of the Act relating to the
abatement of interstate air pollution. Such movement of pollutants
across state lines constitutes interstate commerce subject to the
power granted to Congress by the Constitution to regulate such
commerce.
Whether the originator of the pollution directs it across state
borders unintentionally is immaterial . . . .

69

Defendant argues that pollution has no substantial and harmful effect on commerce, contending that the congressional finding that air pollution has resulted in hazards to air and ground transportation is clearly erroneous, and that if pollution has any effect on air and ground transportation, such effect has been isolated and insubstantial.

. . . Congress, however, concluded that:

> "the growth in the amount and complexity of air pollution brought about by urbanization, industrial development, and the increasing use of motor vehicles, has resulted in mounting dangers to the public health and welfare, including injury to agricultural crops and livestock, damage to and the deterioration of property, and hazards to air and ground transportation." Section 1857d(a)(2).

The finding in section 1857d(a)(2), quoted above is adequately supported by the legislative history.

A court's review of such a congressional finding is limited. The only questions are whether Congress had a rational basis for finding that air pollution affects commerce, and if it had such a basis, whether the means selected to eliminate the evil are appropriate . . . .

Defendant argues that the congressional finding that air pollution has an effect on air and ground transportation is "clearly erroneous" since the legislative history provides only "isolated and insubstantial" interferences with transportation. The power of Congress to regulate activities affecting interstate commerce is to be determined not only by the quantitative effect of individual operations, but also by the total effect of many individual interferences with commerce . . . .

The complaint recites the following findings of fact made by the Hearing Board:

> "3. The malodorous pollution consists of sickening, nauseating and highly offensive odors which are pervasive in effect to the interstate Selbyville, Delaware-Bishop, Maryland area. Such noxious, malodorous air pollution endangers the health and

welfare of persons in the town of Selbyville, Delaware and adjacent and contiguous areas. It causes nausea, sleeplessness, and revulsion, thereby imposing a physiological and psychological burden on persons subjected thereto; and it adversely affects business conditions and property values and impedes industrial development."

. . . .

Malodorous pollution which "adversely affects business conditions and property values and impedes industrial development" would clearly interfere with interstate commerce.

Defendant's argument that there is no economic relationship between the activity regulated and the commerce protected must also fail. As we have seen, Congress undertook to regulate the movement of pollutants across state borders, and it is alleged that those pollutants do interfere with interstate commerce. Hence, the "local activity" (the operation of the rendering plant) is subject to the power of Congress to regulate interstate commerce....

Huron Portland Cement Co. v. Detroit, 362 US 440 (1960)
Mr. Justice Stewart delivered the opinion of the Court.

This appeal from a judgment of the Supreme Court of Michigan draws in question the constitutional validity of certain provisions of Detroit's Smoke Abatement Code as applied to ships owned by the appellant and operated in interstate commerce.

. . . .

In support of the claim that the ordinance cannot constitutionally be applied to appellant's ship, two basic arguments are advanced. First, it is asserted that since the vessels and their equipment, including their boiler, have been inspected, approved and licensed to operate in interstate commerce in accordance with a comprehensive system of regulation enacted by Congress, the City of Detroit may not legislate in such a way as, in effect, to impose additional or inconsistent standards. Secondly, the argument is made that even if Congress has not expressly pre-empted the field, the municipal ordinance "materially affects interstate commerce in matters where uniformity is necessary." We have concluded that neither of these contentions can prevail, and that the Federal Constitution does not prohibit application to the applicant's vessels of the criminal provisions of the Detroit ordinance.

The ordinance was enacted for the manifest purpose of promoting the health and welfare of the city's inhabitants. Legislation designed to free from pollution the very air that people breathe clearly falls within the exercise of even the most traditional concept of what is compendiously known as the police power. In the exercise of that power, the states and their instrumentalities may act, in many areas of interstate commerce and maritime activities, concurrently with the federal government . . . .

The basic limitations upon local legislative power in this area are clear enough. The controlling principles have been reiterated over the years in a host of this Court's decisions. Evenhanded local regulation to effectuate a legitimate local public interest is valid unless pre-empted by federal action, or unduly burdensome on maritime activities or interstate commerce . . . . We conclude that no impermissible burden on commerce has been shown.

U.S. v. Republic Steel, 362 US 482 (1960)
Mr. Justice Douglas delivered the opinion of the Court.

This is a suit by the United States to enjoin respondent companies from depositing industrial solids in the Calumet River (which flows out of Lake Michigan and connects eventually with the Mississippi) without first obtaining a permit from the Chief of Engineers of the Army providing conditions for the removal of the deposits and to order and direct them to restore the depth of the channel to 21 feet by removing portions of existing deposits.

Section 10 of the Rivers and Harbors Act of 1899 . . . provides in part:

> "That the creation of <u>any obstruction</u> not affirmatively authorized by Congress, to the <u>navigable capacity</u> of any of the waters of the United States is hereby prohibited." (italics added)

. . . .

Our conclusions are that the industrial deposits placed by respondents in the Calumet have, on the findings of the District Court, created an "obstruction" within the meaning of #10 of the Act and are discharges not exempt under #13. We also conclude that the District Court was authorized to grant the relief.

The history of federal control over obstructions to the navigable capacity of our rivers and harbors goes back to <u>Williamette Iron Bridge Co. v. Hatch</u>, where the Court held "there is no common law of the United States" which prohibits "obstructions" in our navigable rivers. Congress acted promptly, forbidding by #10 of the Rivers and Harbors Act of 1899 "the creation of any obstruction, not affirmatively authorized by law, to the navigable capacity" of any waters of the United States." . . .

It is argued that "obstruction" means some kind of structure. The design of #10 should be enough to refute that argument, since the ban of "any obstruction," unless approved by Congress, appears in the first part of #10, followed by a semicolon and another provision which bans various kinds of structures unless authorized by the Secretary of the Army.

. . . .

The decision in <u>Sanitary District v. United States</u> seems to us to be decisive. There the Court affirmed a decree enjoining the diversion of water from Lake Michigan through this same river. Mr. Justice Holmes, writing for the Court, did not read #10 narrowly but in the spirit in which Congress moved to fill the gap created by <u>Williamette Iron Bridge Co. v. Hatch</u>. That which affects the water level may, he said, amount to an "obstruction" within the meaning of #10:

> "Evidence is sufficient, if evidence is necessary, to show that a withdrawal of water on the scale directed by the statute of Illinois threatens and will affect the level of the Lakes, and that is a matter which cannot be done without the consent of the United States, even were there no international covenant in the case."

> "There is neither reason nor opportunity for a construction that would not cover the present case. As now applied it concerns a change in the condition of the Lakes and the Chicago River, admitted to be navigable, and if that be necessary, an obstruction to their navigable capacity.... "

It is said that that case is distinguishable because it involved the erections of "structures, " prohibited by the second clause of #10. The "structures" were not "in" navigable waters. The Sanitary District had reversed the flow of the Chicago River, "formerly a little stream flowing into Lake Michigan, " and used it as a sluiceway to draw down the waters of the Great Lakes to a dangerous degree.   Moreover, the Court did not rely on the second clause of #10 but on the first and the third.   The degree in that case did not run against any "structure"; it merely enjoined the diversion of water from Lake Michigan in excess of 250, 000 cubic feet per minute . . . .

The teaching of (this case) is that the term "obstruction" as used in #10 is broad enough to include the diminution of the navigable capacity of a waterway by means not included in the second or third clauses . . . .

We read the 1899 Act charitably in light of the purpose to be served.   The philosophy of the statement by Mr. Justice Holmes . . . that "A river is more than an amenity, it is a treasure, " forbids a narrow, cramped reading of #10 . . . .

New Hampshire v. Atomic Energy Commission, 406 F2d 710 (1969)
Coffin, Circuit Judge

The state of New Hampshire seeks review of an order of the Atomic Energy Commission (AEC), granting a provisional construction permit to the Vermont Yankee Nuclear Power Corporation, organized by ten New England utility companies (applicant), to build a nuclear power reactor at Vernon, Vermont, a site on the Connecticut River, bordering New Hampshire.   The permit was issued at the conclusion of a reactor licensing procedure held under the authority of the Atomic Energy Act of 1954, as amended.

The narrow but important issue is whether the Commission erred in refusing to consider, as outside its regulatory jurisdiction, evidence of possible thermal pollution of the Connecticut River as a result of the discharge of cooling water by applicant's facility. The proposed installation, a "boiling water" reactor, differs from a conventional electric power plant in that the turbine generators which produce the electrical energy are driven by steam derived from the heating of water by the fissioning of uranium in the reactor core. "Thermal pollution" is used to designate the effects on a river--its water, flora, and fauna--of the injection of heated water.

Applicant's application . . . was subjected to review by the Commission's staff, in the course of which eight amendments were added, and by the Advisory Committee on Reactor Safeguards. At the subsequent public hearings before an atomic safety and licensing board, the states of New Hampshire, Vermont and Massachusetts were granted leave to intervene. All three states sought to introduce evidence intended to show that operation of the facility without a cooling tower system for reducing the temperature of water discharged into the river would harm the natural resources of the river. The board issued such evidence inadmissible on the grounds that it related to matters beyond the Commission's jurisdiction, was proscribed by the Commission's Rules of Practice, and was not directed to the issues noticed for hearing . . . . The board concluded that, notwithstanding the possibility that some changes might later be necessary, a provisional construction permit could be issued. It issued its initial decision, finding favorably for applicant on the issues of public health and safety "within the meaning of those terms as authorized by the Commission."

New Hampshire filed exceptions to this decision, contending that the Commission had responsibility for considering the effects of thermal pollution, not only under the Atomic Energy Act of 1954, but also under the Water Quality Act of 1965 and Executive Order 11288. The Commission denied the exceptions, relying on sections of the Atomic Energy Act relating to findings, purpose, and definitions; Congressional statements and subsequent amendments; its own regulations and rules of practice and its own adjudications.

It held that neither the Water Quality Act of 1965 nor Executive Order 11288 were applicable to installations which it did not own or operate.

. . . .

We conclude that the licensing board and the Commission properly refused to consider the proffered evidence of thermal effects. We do so with regret that Congress has not yet established procedures requiring timely and comprehensive consideration of non-radiological pollution effects in the planning of installations to be privately owned and operated. But the very fact that complex questions of jurisdiction among federal agencies, of federal-state relations, of procedure, and even of specialized staff and appropriations must be resolved indicates the inappropriateness of any judicial fiat--particularly when the legislative branch is actively seised of the problem.

One final issue is raised by New Hampshire's argument that the Commission's action has resulted in a taking of property--i.e. use of the Connecticut River--from the citizens of New Hampshire generally without due process and just compensation and for a private as contrasted to a public use. The Commission's response, that the provisional construction permit merely authorizes construction of a facility, that it does not authorize the use of water from the Connecticut River, and that the applicant is not relieved from any obligation to comply with applicable state and federal laws, seems a sufficient one.

Affirmed.

Griggs v. Allegheny County, 369 US 84 (1962)
Mr. Justice Douglas delivered the opinion of the Court.

. . . The question is whether respondent has taken an air easement over petitioner's property for which it must pay just compensation as required by the Fourteenth Amendment.... The Court of Common Pleas, pursuant to customary Pennsylvania procedure, appointed a Board of Viewers to determine whether there had been a "taking" and, if so, the amount due. The Board of Viewers met upon the property; it held a hearing, and in its report

found that there had been a "taking" by respondent of an air easement over petitioner's property and that the compensation payable
(damages suffered) was $12,690. The Court of Common Pleas
dismissed the exceptions of each party to the Board's report. On
appeal, the Supreme Court of Pennsylvania decided, by a divided
vote, that if there were a "taking" in the constitutional sense,
the respondent was not liable.

Respondent owns and maintains the Greater Pittsburgh Airport on land which it purchased to provide airport and air transport facilities. The airport was designed for public use in conformity with the rules and regulations of the Civil Aeronautics
Administration within the scope of the National Airport Plan. . . .

. . . .

The airlines that use the airport are lessees of respondent;
and the leases give them, among other things, the right "to land"
and "take off." No flights were in violation of C.A.A.; nor were
any flights lower than necessary for a safe landing or take-off.
The planes taking off from the northeast runway observed regular
flight patterns ranging from 30 to 300 feet over petitioner's resi-
dence; and on let-down they were within 53 feet to 153 feet.

On take-off the noise of the planes is comparable "to the noise
of a riveting machine or steam hammer." On the let-down the
planes make a noise comparable "to that of a noisy factory." The
Board of Viewers found that "The low altitude flights over plaintiff's property caused the plaintiff and occupants of his property
to become nervous and distraught, eventually causing their removal therefrom as undesirable and unbearable for their residential use."

. . . .

We start with United States v. Causby, which held that the
United States by low flights of its military planes over a chicken
farm made the property unusable for that purpose and that therefore there had been a "taking," in the constitutional sense, of an
air easement for which compensation must be made . . . . Following the decision in the Causby case, Congress redefined "navigable airspace" to mean "airspace above the minimum altitudes

of flight prescribed by regulations issued under this chapter, and shall include airspace needed to insure safety in take-off and landing of aircraft." By the present regulations the "minimum safe altitudes" within the meaning of the statute are defined, so far as relevant here, as heights of 500 feet or 1,000 feet, except where necessary for takeoff or landing." But as we said in the Causby case, the use of land presupposes the use of some of the airspace above it. Otherwise no home could be built, no tree planted, no fence constructed, no chimney erected. An invasion of the "superadjacent airspace" will often "affect the use of the surface of the land itself."

. . . .

The glide path for the northeast runway is as necessary for the operation of the airport as is a surface right of way for operation of a bridge, or as is the land necessary for the operation of a dam . . . . As stated by the Supreme Court of Washington...
" . . . an adequate approach way is as necessary a part of an airport as is the ground on which the airport itself is constructed. . . ."
Without the "approach areas," an airport is indeed not operable. Respondent in designing it had to acquire some private property. Our conclusion is that by constitutional standards it did not acquire enough.
Reversed.

Udall v. Federal Power Commission, 387 US 428 (1967)
Mr. Justice Douglas delivered the opinion of the Court.

The Federal Power Commission has awarded Pacific Northwest Power Company (a joint venture of four private power companies) a license to construct a hydroelectric power project at High Mountain Sheep, a site on the Snake River, a mile upstream from its confluence with the Salmon.
The primary question in the cases involves an interpretation of #7(b) of the Federal Water Power Act of 1920, as amended by the Federal Power Act . . . which provides:

"Whenever, in the judgment of the Commission, the development of any water resources for public purposes should be undertaken by the United States itself, the Commission shall not approve any application for any project affecting such development, but shall cause to be made such examinations, surveys, reports, plans, and estimates of the cost of the proposed development as it may find necessary, and shall submit its findings to Congress with such recommendations as it may find appropriate concerning such development."

The question turns on whether #7(b) requires a showing that licensing of a private, state, or municipal agency is a satisfactory alternative to federal development. We put the question that way because the present record is largely silent on the relative merits of federal and non-federal development . . . .

. . . .

The question whether the proponents of a project "will be able to use" the power supplied is relevant to the issue of the public interest. So too is the regional need for the additional power. But the inquiry should not stop there. A license under the Act empowers the licensee to construct, for its own use and benefit, hydroelectric projects utilizing the flow of navigable waters and thus, in effect, to appropriate water resources, from the public domain. The grant of authority to the Commission to alienate federal water resources does not, of course, turn simply on whether the region will be able to use the additional power. The test is whether the project will be in the public interest. And that determination can be made only after an exploration of all issues relevant to the "public interest," including future power demand and supply, alternative sources of power, the public interest in preserving reaches of wild rivers and wilderness areas, the preservation of anadromous fish for commercial and recreational purposes, and the protection of wildlife.

The need to destroy the river as a waterway, the desirability of its demise, the choices available to satisfy future demands for

for energy--these are all relevant to a decision under #7 and #10 but they were largely untouched by the Commission.

On our remand there should be an exploration of these neglected phases of the cases, as well as the other points raised by the Secretary.

. . . .

It is so ordered.

Scenic Hudson Preservation Conference v. Federal Power Commission, 354 F2d 608 (1965)
Hays, Circuit Judge:

In this proceeding the petitioners are the Scenic Hudson Preservation Conference, an unincorporated association consisting of a number of non-profit conservationist organizations, and the Towns of Cortlandt, Putnam Valley and Yorktown. Petitioners ask us, pursuant to #313(b) of the Federal Power Act, to set aside three orders of the respondent, the Federal Power Commission:

(a) An order of March 9, 1965, granting a license to the intervener, the Consolidated Edison Company of New York, Inc., to construct a pumped storage hydroelectric project on the west side of the Hudson River at Storm King Mountain in Cornwall, New York;

(b) An order of May 6, 1965, denying petitioners' application for a rehearing of the March 9 order, and for the reopening of the proceeding to permit the introduction of additional evidence;

(c) An order of May 6, 1965, denying joint motions filed by the petitioners to expand the scope of supplemental hearings to include consideration of the practicality and cost of underground transmission lines, and of the feasibility of any type of fish protection device.

A pumped storage plant generates electric energy for use during peak load periods, using hydroelectric units driven by water from a headwater pool or reservoir. The contemplated Storm King project would be the largest of its kind in the world.

The Storm King project has aroused grave concern among conservationist groups, adversely affected municipalities and various state and federal legislative units and administrative agencies.

To be licensed by the Commission a prospective project must meet the statutory test of being "best adapted to a comprehensive plan for improving or developing a waterway." . . . In framing the issue before it, the Federal Power Commission properly noted:

"/We/ must compare the Cornwall project with any alternatives that are available. If on this record Con Edison has available an alternative source for meeting its power needs which is better adapted to the development of the Hudson River for all beneficial uses, including scenic beauty, this application should be denied."

If the Commission is properly to discharge its duty in this regard, the record on which it bases its determination must be complete. The petitioners and the public at large have a right to demand this completeness. It is our view, and we find, that the Commission has ignored certain relevant factors and failed to make a thorough study of possible alternatives to the Storm King project. While the courts themselves have no authority to concern themselves with the policies of the Commission, it is their duty to see to it that the Commission's decisions receive that careful consideration which the statute contemplates . . . . Petitioners' application, pursuant to #313(b), 16 U.S.C. #8251(b), to adduce additional evidence is granted. We set aside the three orders of the Commission to which the petition is addressed and remand the case for further proceedings in accordance with this opinion.

. . . .

The Storm King project is located in an area of unique beauty and major historical significance. The highlands and the gorge of the Hudson offer one of the finest pieces of river scenery in the world. The great German traveler Baedecker called it "finer than the Rhine." Petitioners' contention that the Commission must take these factors into consideration in evaluating the Storm King project is justified by the history of the Federal Power Act.

The Federal Water Power Act of 1920 was the outgrowth of a widely supported effort on the part of conservationists to secure the enactment of a complete scheme of national regulation which would promote the comprehensive development of the nation's water resources . . . . .

Congress gave the Federal Power Commission sweeping authority and a specific responsibility . . . . .

Section 10(a) of the Federal Power Act reads:

"#803. Conditions of license generally.
All licenses issued under sections . . . of this
title shall be on the following conditions:

***

(a) That the project adopted, . . . shall be such
as in the judgment of the Commission will be best
adapted to a comprehensive plan for improving
or developing a waterway or waterways for the
use or benefit of interstate or foreign commerce,
for the improvement and utilization of water-power
development, and for other beneficial public uses,
including recreational purposes; . . ."

"Recreational purposes" are expressly included among the beneficial public uses to which the statute refers. The phrase undoubtedly encompasses the conservation of natural resources, the maintenance of natural beauty, and the preservation of historic sites. . . . All of these "beneficial uses," the Supreme Court has observed, "while unregulated, might well be contradictory rather than harmonious," . . .

. . . .

Respondent argues that "petitioners do not have standing to obtain review" because they "make no claim of any personal economic injury resulting from the Commission's action." . . .

The Commission takes a narrow view of the meaning of "aggrieved party" under the Act. The Supreme Court has observed that the law of standing is a "complicated specialty of federal jurisdiction, the solution of whose problems is in any event more or less determined by the specific circumstances of individual situations . . . ." Although a "case" or "controversy" which is otherwise lacking cannot be created by statute, a statute may create new interests or rights and thus give standing to one who would otherwise be barred by the lack of a "case" or "controversy." The "case" or "controversy" requirement of Article III, #2 of the Constitution does not require that an "aggrieved" or "adversely affected" party have a personal economic interest . . . .

The Federal Power Act seeks to protect non-economic as well as economic interests. Indeed, the Commission recognized this in framing the issue in this very case: . . .

> "The project is to be physically located in a general area of our nation steeped in the history of the American Revolution and of the colonial period. It is also a general area of great scenic beauty. The principal issue which must be decided is whether the project's effect on the scenic, historical and recreational values of the area are such that we should deny the application."

In order to insure that the Federal Power Commission will adequately protect the public interest in the aesthetic, conservational, and recreational aspects of power development, those who by their activities and conduct have exhibited a special interest in such areas, must be held to be included in the class of "aggrieved" parties under #313(b). We hold that the Federal Power Act gives petitioners a legal right to protect their special interests . . . .

The licensing order of March 9 and the two orders of May 6 are set aside, and the case remanded for further proceedings.

APPENDIX A

ELEMENTS OF A NATIONAL POLICY
FOR THE ENVIRONMENT

The following language is suggested for a statement of policy, and reflects primarily the proposed position and attitude of the Federal Government, but also could be used for the guidance of State and local governments, private sector industry and commerce, and individual actions. Activities and relationships which involve man and the physical environment (as contrasted with purely person-to-person or person-to-institution relationships) are the subject of this statement.

It is the policy of the United States that:

. Environmental quality and productivity shall be considered in a worldwide context, extending in time from the present to the long-term future.

. Purposeful, intelligent management to recognize and accommodate the conflicting uses of the environment shall be a national responsibility.

. Education shall develop a basis of individual citizen understanding and appreciation of environmental relationships and participation in decisionmaking on these issues.

. Science and technology shall provide management with increased options and capabilities for enhanced productivity and constructive use of the environment.

---

*U.S. Congress. Senate Committee on Interior and Insular Affairs. House Committee on Science and Astronautics. Congressional White Paper on a national policy for the environment, October 1968 (90th Cong., 2d sess., Serial T), pp. 15-16.

The requirement to maintain and enhance long-term productivity and quality of the environment takes precedence over local, short-term usage. This policy recognizes the responsibility to future generations of those presently controlling the development of natural resources and the modification of the living landscape. Although the influence of the U.S. policy will be limited outside of its own borders, the global character of ecological relationships must be the guide for domestic activities. Ecological considerations should be infused into all international relations.

World population and food production must be brought into a controlled balance consistent with a long-term future continuation of a satisfactory standard of living for all.

Energy must be allocated equitably between production and the restoration, maintenance, and enhancement of the environment. Research should focus on solar energy and fusion energy for the long term, and on energy conversion processes with minimum environmental degradation for the short term.

In meeting the objectives of environmental management, it will be necessary to seek the constructive compromise, and resolutely preserve future options.

Priorities and choices among alternatives in environmental manipulation must therefore be planned and managed at the highest level of our political system. All levels of government must require developments within their purview to be in harmony with environmental quality objectives.

Alteration and use of the environment must be planned and controlled rather than left to arbitrary decision. Alternatives must be actively generated and widely discussed. Technological development, introduction of new factors affecting the environment, and modifications of the landscape must be planned to maintain the diversity of plants and animals. Furthermore, such activities should proceed only after an ecological analysis and projection of probable effects. Irreversible or difficultly reversible changes should be accepted only after the most thorough study.

The system of free enterprise democracy must integrate long-term public interests with private economic prosperity. A full range of incentives, inducements, and regulations must be used to link the public interest to the marketplace in an equitable and effective manner.

Manufacturing, processing, and use of natural resources must approach the goal of total recycle to minimize waste control and to sustain materials availability. Renewable resources of air and water must be maintained and enhanced in quality for continued use.

A broad base of technologic, economic, and ecologic information will be necessary. The benefits of preventing quality and productivity deterioration of the environment are now always measurable in the marketplace. Ways must be found to add to cost-benefit analyses nonquantifiable, subjective values for environmental amenities (which cannot be measured in conventional economic terms).

Wherever the maintenance of environmental productivity or the prevention of environmental deterioration cannot be made economical for the private sector, government must find appropriate means of cost-sharing.

Ecological knowledge (data and theories) must be greatly expanded and organized for use in management decisions. Criteria must be established which relate cause and effect in conditions of the environment.

Indicators for all aspects of environmental productivity and quality must be developed and continuously measured to provide a feedback to management. In particular, the environmental amenities (recreational, esthetic, psychic) must be evaluated. Social sciences must be supported to provide relevant and dependable interpretation of information for environmental management.

Standards of quality must not be absolute--rather, they should be chosen after balancing all criteria against the total demands of society. Standards will vary with locality, must be adjusted from time to time, and we must develop our capabilities accordingly.

Decisions to make new technological applications must include consideration of unintended, unanticipated, and unwanted consequences. Technology should be directed to ameliorating these effects so that the benefits of applied science are retained.

Public awareness of environmental quality relationships to human welfare must be increased. Education at all levels should include an appreciation of mankind's harmony with the environment. A literacy as to environmental matters must be built up in the public mind. The ultimate responsibility for improved maintenance and control of the environment rests with the individual citizen.

THE NATIONAL ENVIRONMENTAL POLICY ACT OF 1969
PUBLIC LAW 91-190, JANUARY 1, 1970

AN ACT to establish a national policy for the environment, to provide for the establishment of a Council on Environmental Quality, and for other purposes

Be it enacted by the Senate and House of Representatives of the United States of America in Congress assembled, That this Act may be cited as the "National Environmental Policy Act of 1969."

PURPOSE

SEC. 2. The purposes of this Act are: To declare a national policy which will encourage productive and enjoyable harmony between man and his environment; to promote efforts which will prevent or eliminate damage to the environment and biosphere and stimulate the health and welfare of man; to enrich the understanding of the ecological systems and natural resources important to the Nation; and to establish a Council on Environmental Quality.

TITLE I

DECLARATION OF A NATIONAL ENVIRONMENTAL POLICY

SEC. 101. (a) The Congress, recognizing the profound impact of man's activity on the interrelations of all components of the natural environment, particularly the profound influences of population growth, high-density urbanization, industrial expansion, resource exploitation, and new and expanding technological advances and recognizing further the critical importance of restoring and maintaining environmental quality to the overall welfare and development of man, declares that it is the continuing policy of the Federal Government, in cooperation with State and local governments, and other public and private organizations, to use all practicable means and measures, including financial and technical assistance, in a manner calculated to foster and promote the general welfare, to create and maintain conditions under which man and nature can exist in productive harmony, and fulfill the social, economic, and other requirements of present and future generations of Americans.

(b) In order to carry out the policy set forth in this Act, it is the continuing responsibility of the Federal Government to use all practicable means, consistent with other essential considerations of national policy, to improve and coordinate Federal plans, functions, programs, and resources to the end that the Nation may--

(1) fulfill the responsibilities of each generation as trustee of the environment for succeeding generations;

(2) assure for all Americans safe, healthful, productive, and esthetically and culturally pleasing surroundings;

(3) attain the widest range of beneficial uses of the environment without degradation, risk to health or safety, or other undesirable and unintended consequences;

(4) preserve important historic, cultural, and natural aspects of our national heritage, and maintain, wherever possible, an environment which supports diversity, and variety of individual choice;

(5) achieve a balance between population and resource use which will permit high standards of living and a wide sharing of life's amenities; and

(6) enhance the quality of renewable resources and approach the maximum attainable recycling of depletable resources.

(c) The Congress recognizes that each person should enjoy a healthful environment and that each person has a responsibility to contribute to the preservation and enhancement of the environment.

SEC. 102. The Congress authorizes and directs that, to the fullest extent possible: (1) the policies, regulations, and public laws of the United States shall be interpreted and administered in accordance with the policies set forth in this Act, and (2) all agencies of the Federal Government shall--

(A) utilize a systematic, interdisciplinary approach which will insure the integrated use of the natural and social sciences and the environmental design arts in planning and in decisionmaking which may have an impact on man's environment;

(B) identify and develop methods and procedures, in consultation with the Council on Environmental Quality established by title II of this Act, which will insure that presently unquantified environmental amenities and values may be given appropriate consideration in decisionmaking along with economic and technical considerations;

(C) include in every recommendation or report on proposals for legislation and other major Federal actions significantly affecting the quality of the human environment, a detailed statement by the responsible official on--

(i) the environmental impact of the proposed action,

(ii) any adverse environmental effects which cannot be avoided should the proposal be implemented,

(iii) alternatives to the proposed action,

(iv) the relationship between local short-term uses of man's environment and the maintenance and enhancement of long-term productivity, and

(v) any irreversible and irretrievable commitments of resources which would be involved in the proposed action should it be implemented.

Prior to making any detailed statement, the responsible Federal official shall consult with and obtain the comments of any Federal agency which has jurisdiction by law or special expertise with respect to any environmental impact involved. Copies of such statement and the comments and views of the appropriate Federal, State, and local agencies, which are authorized to develop and enforce environmental standards, shall be made available to the President, the Council on Environmental Quality and to the public as provided by section 552 of title 5, United States Code, and shall accompany the proposal through the existing agency review processes;

(D) study, develop, and describe appropriate alternatives to recommended courses of action in any proposal which involves unresolved conflicts concerning alternative uses of available resources;

(E) recognize the worldwide and long-range character of environmental problems and, where consistent with the foreign policy of the United States, lend appropriate support to initiatives, resolutions, and programs designed to maximize international cooperation in anticipating and preventing a decline in the quality of mankind's world environment;

(F) make available to States, counties, municipalities, institutions, and individuals, advice and information useful in restoring, maintaining, and enhancing the quality of the environment;

(G) initiate and utilize ecological information in the planning and development of resource-oriented projects, and

(H) assist the Council on Environmental Quality established by title II of this Act.

SEC. 103. All agencies of the Federal Government shall review their present statutory authority, administrative regulations, and current policies and procedures for the purpose of determining whether there are any deficiencies or inconsistencies therein which prohibit full compliance with the purposes and provisions of this Act and shall propose to the President not later than July 1, 1971, such measures as may be necessary to bring their authority and policies into conformity with the intent, purposes, and procedures set forth in this Act.

SEC. 104. Nothing in section 102 or 103 shall in any way affect the specific statutory obligations of any Federal agency (1) to comply with criteria or standards of environmental quality, (2) to coordinate or consult with any other Federal or State agency, or (3) to act, or refrain from acting contingent upon the recommendations or certification of any other Federal or State agency.

SEC. 105. The policies and goals set forth in this Act are supplementary to those set forth in existing authorizations of Federal agencies.

TITLE II

COUNCIL ON ENVIRONMENTAL QUALITY

SEC. 201. The President shall transmit to the Congress annually beginning July 1, 1970, an Environmental Quality Report (hereinafter referred to as the "report") which shall set forth (1) the status and condition of the major natural, manmade, or altered environmental classes of the Nation, including, but not limited to, the air, the aquatic, including marine, estuarine, and fresh water, and the terrestrial environment, including, but not limited to, the forest, dryland, wetland, range, urban, suburban, and rural environment; (2) current and foreseeable trends in the quality, management and utilization of such environments and the effects of those trends on the social, economic, and other requirements of the Nation; (3) the adequacy of available natural resources for fulfilling human and economic requirements of the Nation in the light of expected population pressures; (4) a review of the programs and activities (including regulatory activities) of the Federal Government, the State and local governments, and nongovernmental entities or individuals, with particular reference to their effect on the environment and on the conservation, development and utilization of natural resources; and (5) a program for remedying the deficiencies of existing programs and activities, together with recommendations for legislation.

SEC. 202. There is created in the Executive Office of the President a Council on Environmental Quality (hereinafter referred to as the "Council"). The Council shall be composed of three members who shall be appointed by the President to serve at his pleasure, by and with the advice and consent of the Senate. The President shall designate one of the members of the Council to serve as Chairman. Each member shall be a person who, as a result of his training, experience, and attainments, is exceptionally well qualified to analyze and interpret environmental trends and information of all kinds; to appraise programs and activities of the Federal Government in the light of the policy set forth in title I of this Act; to be conscious of and responsible to the scientific, economic, social, esthetic, and cultural needs and interests of the Nation; and to formulate and recommend national policies to promote the improvement of the quality of the environment.

SEC. 203. The Council may employ such officers and employees as may be necessary to carry out its functions under this Act. In addition, the Council may employ and fix the compensation of such experts and consultants as may be necessary for the carrying out of its functions under this Act, in accordance with section 3109 of title 5, United States Code (but without regard to the last sentence thereof).

SEC. 204. It shall be the duty and function of the Council--

(1) to assist and advise the President in the preparation of the Environmental Quality Report required by section 201;

(2) to gather timely and authoritative information concerning the conditions and trends in the quality of the environment both current and prospective, to analyze and interpret such information for the purpose of determining whether such conditions and trends are interfering, or are likely to interfere, with the achievement of the policy set forth in title I of this Act, and to compile and submit to the President studies relating to such conditions and trends;

(3) to review and appraise the various programs and activities of the Federal Government in the light of the policy set forth in title I of this Act for the purpose of determining the extent to which such programs and activities are contributing to the achievement of such policy, and to make recommendations to the President with respect thereto;

(4) to develop and recommend to the President national policies to foster and promote the improvement of environmental quality to meet the conservation, social, economic, health, and other requirements and goals of the Nation;

(5) to conduct investigations, studies, surveys, research, and analyses relating to ecological systems and environmental quality;

(6) to document and define changes in the natural environment, including the plant and animal systems, and to accumulate necessary data and other information for a continuing analysis of these changes or trends and an interpretation of their underlying causes;

(7) to report at least once each year to the President on the state and condition of the environment; and

(8) to make and furnish such studies, reports thereon, and recommendations with respect to matters of policy and legislation as the President may request.

SEC. 205. In exercising its powers, functions, and duties under this act, the Council shall--

(1) consult with the Citizens'Advisory Committee on Environmental Quality established by Executive Order numbered 11472, dated May 29, 1969, and with such representatives of

science, industry, agriculture, labor, conservation organizations, State and local governments and other groups, as it deems advisable; and

(2) utilize, to the fullest extent possible, the services, facilities, and information (including statistical information) of public and private agencies and organizations and individuals, in order that duplication of effort and expense may be avoided, thus assuring that the Council's activities will not unnecessarily overlap or conflict with similar activities authorized by law and performed by established agencies.

SEC. 206. Members of the Council shall serve full time and the Chairman of the Council shall be compensated at the rate provided for Level II of the Executive Schedule Pay Rates (5 U.S.C. 5313). The other members of the Council shall be compensated at the rate provided for Level IV of the Executive Schedule Pay Rates (5 U.S.C. 5315).

SEC. 207. There are authorized to be appropriated to carry out the provisions of this Act not to exceed $300,000 for fiscal year 1970, $700,000 for fiscal year 1971, and $1,000,000 for each fiscal year thereafter.

Approved January 1, 1970.

THE ENVIRONMENTAL QUALITY IMPROVEMENT ACT OF 1970, PUBLIC LAW 91-224, APRIL 3, 1970

TITLE II--ENVIRONMENTAL QUALITY
(of the Water Quality Improvement Act of 1970)

SHORT TITLE

SEC. 201. This title may be cited as the "Environmental Quality Improvement Act of 1970."

FINDINGS, DECLARATIONS, AND PURPOSES

SEC. 202. (a) The Congress finds--

(1) that man has caused changes in the environment;

(2) that many of these changes may affect the relationship between man and his environment; and

(3) that population increases and urban concentration contribute directly to pollution and the degradation of our environment.

(b) (1) The Congress declares that there is a national policy for the environment which provides for the enhancement of environmental quality. This policy is evidenced by statutes heretofore enacted relating to the prevention, abatement, and control of environmental pollution, water and land resources, transportation, and economic and regional development.

(2) The primary responsibility for implementing this policy rests with State and local governments.

(3) The Federal Government encourages and supports implementation of this policy through appropriate regional organizations established under existing law.

(c) The purposes of this title are--

(1) to assure that each Federal department and agency conducting or supporting public works activities which affect

the environment shall implement the policies established under existing law; and

(2) to authorize an Office of Environmental Quality, which, notwithstanding any other provision of law, shall provide the professional and administrative staff for the Council on Environmental Quality established by Public Law 91-190.

OFFICE OF ENVIRONMENTAL QUALITY

SEC. 203. (a) There is established in the Executive Office of the President an office to be known as the Office of Environmental Quality (hereafter in this title referred to as the "Office"). The Chairman of the Council on Environmental Quality established by Public Law 91-190 shall be the Director of the Office. There shall be in the Office a Deputy Director who shall be appointed by the President, by and with the advice and consent of the Senate.

(b) The compensation of the Deputy Director shall be fixed by the President at a rate not in excess of the annual rate of compensation payable to the Deputy Director of the Bureau of the Budget.

(c) The Director is authorized to employ such officers and employees (including experts and consultants) as may be necessary to enable the Office to carry out its functions under this title and Public Law 91-190, except that he may employ no more than ten specialists and other experts without regard to the provisions of title 5, United States Code, governing appointments in the competitive service, and pay such specialists and experts without regard to the provisions of chapter 51 and the subchapter 111 of chapter 53 of such title relating to classification and General Schedule pay rates, but no such specialist or expert shall be paid at a rate in excess of the maximum rate for GS-18 of the General Schedule under section 5330 of title 5.

(d) In carrying out his functions the Director shall assist and advise the President on policies and programs of the Federal Government affecting environmental quality by--

(1) providing the professional and administrative staff and support for the Council on Environmental Quality established by Public Law 91-190;

(2) assisting the Federal agencies and departments in appraising the effectiveness of existing and proposed facilities,

programs, policies, and activities of the Federal Government, and those specific major projects designated by the President which do not require individual project authorization by Congress, which affect environmental quality;

(3) reviewing the adequacy of existing systems for monitoring and predicting environmental changes in order to achieve effective coverage and efficient use of research facilities and other resources;

(4) promoting the advancement of scientific knowledge of the effects of actions and technology on the environment and encourage the development of the means to prevent or reduce adverse effects that endanger the health and well-being of man;

(5) assisting in coordinating among the Federal departments and agencies those programs and activities which affect, protect, and improve environmental quality;

(6) assisting the Federal departments and agencies in the development and interrelationship of environmental quality criteria and standards established through the Federal Government;

(7) collecting, collating, analyzing, and interpreting data and information on environmental quality, ecological research, and evaluation.

(e) The Director is authorized to contract with public or private agencies, institutions, and organizations and with individuals without regard to sections 3618 and 3709 of the Revised Statutes (31 U.S.C. 529, 41 U.S.C. 5) in carrying out his functions.

REPORT

SEC. 204. Each Environmental Quality Report required by Public Law 91-190 shall, upon transmittal to Congress, be referred to each standing committee having jurisdiction over any part of the subject matter of the Report.

APPENDIX D

THE PRESIDENT

Executive Order 11472
ESTABLISHING THE ENVIRONMENTAL QUALITY COUNCIL
AND THE CITIZENS' ADVISORY COMMITTEE
ON ENVIRONMENTAL QUALITY

By virtue of the authority vested in me as President of the United States, it is ordered as follows:

PART I. ENVIRONMENTAL QUALITY COUNCIL

SECTION 101. Establishment of the Council. (a) There is hereby established the Environmental Quality Council (hereinafter referred to as "the Council").

(b) The President of the United States shall preside over meetings of the Council. The Vice President shall preside in the absence of the President.

(c) The Council shall be composed of the following members:

The Vice President of the United States
Secretary of Agriculture
Secretary of Commerce
Secretary of Health, Education and Welfare
Secretary of Housing and Urban Development
Secretary of the Interior
Secretary of Transportation

and such other heads of departments and agencies and others as the President may from time to time direct.

(d) Each member of the Council may designate an alternate, who shall serve as a member of the Council whenever the regular member is unable to attend any meeting of the council.

(e) When matters which affect the interest of Federal agencies the heads of which are not members of the Council are to be considered by the Council, the President or his representative may invite such agency heads or their alternates to participate in the deliberations of the Council.

(f) The Director of the Bureau of the Budget, the Chairman of the Council of Economic Advisers, and the Executive Secretary of the Council for Urban Affairs or their representatives may participate in the deliberations of the Environmental Quality Council as observers.

(g) The Science Adviser to the President shall be Executive Secretary of the Council and shall assist the President in directing the affairs of the Council.

SEC. 102. Functions of the Council. (a) The Council shall advise and assist the President with respect to environmental quality matters and shall perform such other related duties as the President may from time to time prescribe. In addition thereto, the Council is directed to:

(1) Recommend measures to ensure that Federal policies and programs, including those for development and conservation of natural resources, take adequate account of environmental effects.

(2) Review the adequacy of existing systems for monitoring and predicting environmental changes so as to achieve effective coverage and efficient use of facilities and other resources.

(3) Foster cooperation between the Federal Government, State and local governments, and private organizations in environmental programs.

(4) Seek advancement of scientific knowledge of changes in the environment and encourage the development of technology to prevent or minimize adverse effects that endanger man's health and well-being.

(5) Stimulate public and private participation in programs and activities to protect against pollution of the Nation's air, water, and land and its living resources.

(6) Encourage timely public disclosure by all levels of government and by private parties of plans that would affect the quality of the environment.

(7) Assure assessment of new and changing technologies for their potential effects on the environment.

(8) Facilitate coordination among departments and agencies of the Federal Government in protecting and improving the environment.

(b) The Council shall review plans and actions of Federal agencies affecting outdoor recreation and natural beauty. The Council may conduct studies and make recommendations to the President on matters of policy in the fields of outdoor recreation and natural beauty. In carrying out the foregoing provisions of this subsection, the Council shall, as far as may be practical, advise Federal agencies with respect to the effect of their respective plans and programs on recreation and natural beauty, and may suggest to such agencies ways to accomplish the purposes of this order. For the purposes of this order, plans and programs may include, but are not limited to, those for or affecting: (1) Development, restoration, and preservation of the beauty of the countryside, urban and suburban areas, water resources, wild rivers, scenic roads, parkways and highways, (2) the protection and appropriate management of scenic or primitive areas, natural wonders, historic sites, and recreation areas, (3) the management of Federal land and water resources, including fish and wildlife, to enhance natural beauty and recreational opportunities consistent with other essential uses, (4) cooperation with the States and their local subdivisions and private organizations and individuals in areas of mutual interest, (5) interstate arrangements, including Federal participation where authorized and necessary, and (6) leadership in a nationwide recreation and beautification effort.

(c) The Council shall assist the President in preparing periodic reports to the Congress on the subjects of this order.

SEC. 103. Coordination. The Secretary of the Interior may make available to the Council for coordination of outdoor recreation the authorities and resources available to him under the Act of May 28, 1963, 77 Stat. 49; to the extent permitted by law, he may make such authorities and resources available to the Council also for promoting such coordination of other matters assigned to the Council by this order.

SEC. 104. Assistance for the Council. In compliance with provisions of applicable law, and as necessary to serve the purposes of this order, (1) the Office of Science and Technology shall provide or arrange for necessary administrative and staff services, support, and facilities for the Council, and (2) each department and agency which has membership on the Council under Section 101 (c) hereof shall furnish the Council such information and other assistance as may be available.

PART II. CITIZENS' ADVISORY COMMITTEE
ON ENVIRONMENTAL QUALITY

SEC. 201. Establishment of the Committee. There is hereby established the Citizens' Advisory Committee on Environmental Quality (hereinafter referred to as the "Committee"). The Committee shall be composed of a chairman and not more than 14 other members appointed by the President. Appointments to membership on the Committee shall be for staggered terms, except that the chairman of the Committee shall serve until his successor is appointed.

SEC. 202. Functions of the Committee. The Committee shall advise the President and the Council of matters assigned to the Council by the provisions of this order.

SEC. 203. Expenses. Members of the Committee shall receive no compensation from the United States by reasons of their services but shall be entitled to receive travel and expenses, including per diem in lieu of subsistence, as authorized by law (5 U.S.C. 5701-5708) for persons in the Government service employed intermittently.

SEC. 204. Continuity. Persons who on the date of this order are members of the Citizens' Advisory Committee on Recreation and Natural Beauty established by Executive Order No. 11278 of May 4, 1966, as amended, shall, until the expirations of their respective terms and without further action by the President, be members of the Committee established by the provisions of this Part in lieu of an equal number of the members provided for in section 201 of this order.

PART III. GENERAL PROVISIONS

SEC. 301. Construction. Nothing in this order shall be construed as subjecting any department, establishment, or other instrumentality of the executive branch of the Federal Government or the head thereof, or any function vested by law in or assigned persuant to law to any such agency or head, to the authority of any other such agency or head or as abrogating, modifying, or restricting any such function in any manner.

SEC. 302. Prior bodies and orders. The President's Council on Recreation and Natural Beauty and the Citizens' Advisory

Committee on Recreation and Natural Beauty are hereby terminated and the following are revoked:

(1) Executive Order No. 11278 of May 4, 1966.

(2) Executive Order No. 11359A of June 29, 1967.

(3) Executive Order No. 11402 of March 29, 1968.

RICHARD NIXON

THE WHITE HOUSE,
    May 29, 1969.

(F. R. Doc. 69-6572; Filed, May 29, 1969; 4:10 p.m.)

APPENDIX E

Executive Order 11507
PREVENTION, CONTROL, AND ABATEMENT OF
AIR AND WATER POLLUTION AT FEDERAL FACILITIES
February 4, 1970

By virtue of the authority vested in me as President of the United States and in furtherance of the purpose and policy of the Clean Air Act, as amended (42 U.S.C. 1857), the Federal Water Pollution Control Act, as amended (33 U.S.C. 466), and the National Environmental Policy Act of 1969 (Public Law No. 91-190, approved January 1, 1970), it is ordered as follows:

SECTION 1. Policy. It is the intent of this order that the Federal Government in the design, operation, and maintenance of its facilities shall provide leadership in the nationwide effort to protect and enhance the quality of our air and water resources.

SEC. 2. Definitions. As used in this order:

(a) The term "respective Secretary" shall mean the Secretary of Health, Education, and Welfare in matters pertaining to air pollution control and the Secretary of the Interior in matters pertaining to water pollution control.

(b) The term "agencies" shall mean the departments, agencies, and establishments of the executive branch.

(c) The term "facilities" shall mean the buildings, installations, structures, public works, equipment, aircraft, vessels, and other vehicles and property, owned by or constructed or manufactured for the purpose of leasing to the Federal Government.

(d) The term "air and water quality standards" shall mean respectively the quality standards and related plans of implementation, including emission standards, adopted pursuant to the Clean Air Act, as amended, and the Federal Water Pollution Control Act, as amended, or as prescribed pursuant to section 4(b) of this order.

(e) The term "performance specifications" shall mean permissible limits of emissions, discharges, or other values applicable

103

to a particular Federal facility that would, as a minimum, provide for conformance with air and water quality standards as defined herein.

(f) The term "United States" shall mean the fifty States, the District of Columbia, the Commonwealth of Puerto Rico, the Virgin Islands, and Guam.

SEC. 3. Responsibilities. (a) Heads of agencies shall, with regard to all facilities under their jurisdiction.

(1) Maintain review and surveillance to ensure that the standards set forth in section 4 of this order are met on a continuing basis.

(2) Direct particular attention to identifying potential air and water quality problems associated with the use and production of new materials and make provisions for their prevention and control.

(3) Consult with the respective Secretary concerning the best techniques and methods available for the protection and enhancement of air and water quality.

(4) Develop and publish procedures, within six months of the date of this order, to ensure that the facilities under their jurisdiction are in conformity with this order. In the preparation of such procedures there shall be timely and appropriate consultation with the respective Secretary.

(b) The respective Secretary shall provide leadership in implementing this order, including the provision of technical advice and assistance to the heads of agencies in connection with their duties and responsibilities under this order.

(c) The Council on Environmental Quality shall maintain continuing review of the implementation of this order and shall, from time to time, report to the President thereon.

SEC. 4. Standards. (a) Heads of agencies shall ensure that all facilities under their jurisdiction are designed, operated, and maintained so as to meet the following requirements:

(1) Facilities shall conform to air and water quality standards as defined in section 2(d) of this order. In those cases where no such air or water quality standards are in force for a particular geographical area, Federal facilities in that area shall conform to the standards established pursuant to subsection (b) of this section. Federal facilities shall also conform to the performance specifications provided for in this order.

104

(2) Actions shall be taken to avoid or minimize wastes created through the complete cycle of operations of each facility.

(3) The use of municipal or regional waste collection or disposal systems shall be the preferred method of disposal of wastes from Federal facilities. Whenever use of such a system is not feasible or appropriate, the heads of agencies concerned shall take necessary measures for the satisfactory disposal of such wastes, including:

(A) When appropriate, the installation and operation of their own waste treatment and disposal facilities in a manner consistent with this section.

(B) The provision of trained manpower, laboratory and other supporting facilities as appropriate to meet the requirements of this section.

(C) The establishment of requirements that operators of Federal pollution control facilities meet levels of proficiency consistent with the operator certification requirements of the State in which the facility is located. In the absence of such State requirements the respective Secretary may issue guidelines, pertaining to operator qualifications and performance, for the use of heads of agencies.

(4) The use, storage, and handline of all materials, including but not limited to, solid fuels, ashes, petroleum products, and other chemical and biological agents, shall be carried out so as to avoid or minimize the possibilities for water and air pollution. When appropriate, preventive measures shall be taken to entrap spillage or discharge or otherwise to prevent accidental pollution. Each agency, in consultation with the respective Secretary, shall establish appropriate emergency plans and procedures for dealing with accidental pollution.

(5) No waste shall be disposed of or discharged in such a manner as could result in the pollution of ground water which would endanger the health or welfare of the public.

(6) Discharges of radioactivity shall be in accordance with the applicable rules, regulations, or requirements of the Atomic Energy Commission and with the policies and guidance of the Federal Radiation Council as published in the Federal Register.

(b) In those cases where there are no air or water quality standards as defined in section 2(d) of this order in force for a particular geographic area or in those cases where more stringent requirements are deemed advisable for Federal facilities, the respective Secretary, in consultation with appropriate Federal, State, interstate, and local agencies, may issue regulations establishing air or water quality standards for the purpose of this order, including related schedules for implementation.

(c) The heads of agencies, in consultation with the respective Secretary, may from time to time identify facilities or uses thereof which are to be exempted, including temporary relief, from provisions of this order in the interest of national security or in extraordinary cases where it is in the national interest. Such exemptions shall be reviewed periodically by the respective Secretary and the heads of the agencies concerned. A report on exemptions granted shall be submitted to the Council on Environmental Quality periodically.

SEC. 5. <u>Procedures for abatement of air wnd water pollution at existing Federal facilities</u>. (a) Actions necessary to meet the requirements of subsections (a)(1) and (b) of section 4 of this order pertaining to air and water pollution at existing facilities are to be completed or under way no later than December 31, 1972. In cases where an enforcement conference called pursuant to law or air and water quality standards require earlier actions, the earlier date shall be applicable.

(b) In order to ensure full compliance with the requirements of section 5(a) and to facilitate budgeting for necessary corrective and preventive measures, heads of agencies shall present to the Director of the Bureau of the Budget by June 30, 1970, a plan to provide for such improvements as may be necessary to meet the required date. Subsequent revisions needed to keep any such plan up-to-date shall be promptly submitted to the Director of the Bureau of the Budget.

(c) Heads of agencies shall notify the respective Secretary as to the performance specifications proposed for each facility to meet the requirements of subsections (a)(1) and (b) of section 4 of this order. Where the respective Secretary finds that such performance specifications are not adequate to meet such requirements, he shall consult with the agency head and the latter shall thereupon develop adequate performance specifications.

(d) As may be found necessary, heads of agencies may submit requests to the Director of the Bureau of the Budget for extensions of time for a project beyond the time specified in section 5(a). The Director, in consultation with the respective Secretary, may approve such request if the Director deems that such project is not technically feasible or immediately necessary to meet the requirements of subsections 4(a) and (b). Full justification as to the extraordinary circumstances necessitating any such extension shall be required.

(e) Heads of agencies shall not use for any other purpose any of the amounts appropriated and apportioned for corrective and preventive measures necessary to meet the requirements of subsection (a) for the fiscal year ending June 30, 1970, and for any subsequent fiscal year.

SEC. 6. Procedures for new Federal facilities. (a) Heads of agencies shall ensure that the requirements of section 4 of this order are considered at the earliest possible stage of planning for new facilities.

(b) A request for funds to defray the cost of designing and constructing new facilities in the United States shall be included in the annual budget estimates of an agency only if such request includes funds to defray the costs of such measures as may be necessary to assure that the new facility will meet the requirements of section 4 of this order.

(c) Heads of agencies shall notify the respective Secretary as to the performance specifications proposed for each facility when action is necessary to meet the requirements of subsections (a)(1) and (b) of section 4 of this order. Where the respective Secretary finds that such performance specifications are not adequate to meet such requirements he shall consult with the agency head and the latter shall thereupon develop adequate performance specifications.

(d) Heads of agencies shall give due consideration to the quality of air and water resources when facilities are constructed or operated outside the United States.

SEC. 7. Procedures for Federal water resources projects.

(a) All water resources projects of the Departments of Agriculture, the Interior, and the Army, the Tennessee Valley Authority, and the United States Section of the International Boundary and Water Commission shall be consistent with the requirements

107

of section 4 of this order. In addition, all such projects shall be presented for the consideration of the Secretary of the Interior at the earliest feasible stage if they involve proposals or recommendations with respect to the authorization or construction of any Federal water resources project in the United States. The Secretary of the Interior shall review plans and supporting data for all such projects relating to water quality, and shall prepare a report to the head of the responsible agency describing the potential impact of the project on water quality, including recommendations concerning any changes or other measures with respect thereto which he considers to be necessary in connection with the design, construction, and operation of the project.

(b) The report of the Secretary of the Interior shall accompany at the earliest practicable stage any report proposing authorization or construction, or a request for funding, of such a water resource project. In any case in which the Secretary of the Interior fails to submit a report within 90 days after receipt of project plans, the head of the agency concerned may propose authorization, construction, or funding of the project without such an accompanying report. In such a case, the head of the agency concerned shall explicitly state in his request or report concerning the project that the Secretary of the Interior has not reported on the potential impact of the project on water quality.

SEC. 8. Saving provisions. Except to the extent that they are inconsistent with this order, all outstanding rules, regulations, orders, delegations, or other forms of administrative action issued, made, or otherwise taken under the orders superseded by section 9 hereof or relating to the subject of this order shall remain in full force and effect until amended, modified, or terminated by proper authority.

SEC. 9. Orders superseded. Executive Order No. 11282 of May 26, 1966, and Executive Order No. 11288 of July 2, 1966, are hereby superseded.

RICHARD NIXON.

THE WHITE HOUSE

108

THE PRESIDENT

Executive Order 11514
PROTECTION AND ENHANCEMENT OF ENVIRONMENTAL QUALITY

By virtue of the authority vested in me as President of the United States and in furtherance of the purpose and policy of the National Environmental Policy Act of 1969 (Public Law No. 91-190, approved January 1, 1970), it is ordered as follows:

SECTION 1. Policy. The Federal Government shall provide leadership in protecting and enhancing the quality of the Nation's environment to sustain and enrich human life. Federal agencies shall initiate measures needed to direct their policies, plans and programs so as to meet national environmental goals. The Council on Environmental Quality, through the Chairman, shall advise and assist the President in leading this national effort.

SEC. 2. Responsibilities of Federal agencies. Consonant with Title I of the National Environmental Policy Act of 1969, hereafter referred to as the "Act", the heads of Federal agencies shall:

(a) Monitor, evaluate, and control on a continuing basis their agencies' activities so as to protect and enhance the quality of the environment. Such activities shall include those directed to controlling pollution and enhancing the environment and those designed to accomplish other program objectives which may affect the quality of the environment. Agencies shall develop programs and measures to protect and enhance environmental quality and shall assess progress in meeting the specific objectives of such activities. Heads of agencies shall consult with appropriate Federal, State and local agencies in carrying out their activities as they affect the quality of the environment.

(b) Develop procedures to ensure the fullest practicable provision of timely public information and understanding of Federal plans and programs with environmental impact in order to obtain the views of interested parties. These procedures shall include, whenever appropriate, provision for public hearings, and shall provide the public with relevant information, including information on alternative courses of action. Federal agencies shall also encourage State and local agencies to adopt similar procedures for informing the public concerning their activities affecting the quality of the environment.

(c) Insure that information regarding existing or potential environmental problems and control methods developed as part of research, development, demonstration, test, or evaluation activities is made available to Federal agencies, States, counties, municipalities, institutions, and other entities, as appropriate.

(d) Review their agencies' statutory authority, administrative regulations, policies, and procedures, including those relating to loans, grants, contracts, leases, licenses, or permits, in order to identify any deficiencies or inconsistencies therein which prohibit or limit full compliance with the purposes and provisions of the Act. A report on this review and the corrective actions taken or planned, including such measures to be proposed to the President as may be necessary to bring their authority and policies into conformance with the intent, purposes, and procedures of the Act, shall be provided to the Council on Environmental Quality not later than September 1, 1970.

(e) Engage in exchange of data and research results, and cooperate with agencies of other governments to foster the purposes of the Act.

(f) Proceed, in coordination with other agencies, with actions required by section 102 of the Act.

SEC. 3. Responsibilities of Council on Environmental Quality. The Council on Environmental Quality shall:

(a) Evaluate existing and proposed policies and activities of the Federal Government directed to the control of pollution and the enhancement of the environment and to the accomplishment of other objectives which affect the quality of the environment. This shall include continuing review of procedures employed in the development and enforcement of Federal standards affecting environmental quality. Based upon such evaluations the Council shall, where appropriate, recommend to the President policies and programs to achieve more effective protection and enhancement of environmental quality and shall, where appropriate, seek resolution of significant environmental issues.

(b) Recommend to the President and to the agencies priorities among programs designed for the control of pollution and for enhancement of the environment.

(c) Determine the need for new policies and programs for dealing with environmental problems not being adequately addressed.

(d) Conduct, as it determines to be appropriate, public hearings or conferences on issues of environmental significance.

(e) Promote the development and use of indices and monitoring systems (1) to assess environmental conditions and trends, (2) to predict the environmental impact of proposed public and private actions, and (3) to determine the effectiveness of programs for protecting and enhancing environmental quality.

(f) Coordinate Federal programs related to environmental quality.

(g) Advise and assist the President and the agencies in achieving international cooperation for dealing with environmental problems, under the foreign policy guidance of the Secretary of State.

(h) Issue guidelines to Federal agencies for the preparation of detailed statements on proposals for legislation and other Federal actions affecting the environment, as required by section 102(2)(C) of the Act.

(i) Issue such other instructions to agencies, and request such reports and other information from them, as may be required to carry out the Council's responsibilities under the Act.

(j) Assist the President in preparing the annual Environmental Quality Report provided for in section 201 of the Act.

(k) Foster investigations, studies, surveys, research, and analyses relating to (i) ecological systems and environmental quality, (ii) the impact of new and changing technologies thereon, and (iii) means of preventing or reducing adverse effects from such technologies.

SEC. 4. Amendments of E. O. 11472. Executive Order No. 11472 of May 29, 1969, including the heading thereof, is hereby amended:

(1) By substituting for the term "the Environmental Quality Council", wherever it occurs, the following: "the Cabinet Committee on the Environment".

(2) By substituting for the term "the Council", wherever it occurs, the following: "the Cabinet Committee".

111

(3) By inserting in subsection (f) of section 101, after "Budget, ", the following: "the Director of the Office of Science and Technology, ".

(4) By substituting for subsection (g) of section 101 the following:

"(g) The Chairman of the Council on Environmental Quality (established by Public Law 91-190) shall assist the President in directing the affairs of the Cabinet Committee."

(5) By deleting subsection (c) of section 102.

(6) By substituting for "the Office of Science and Technology", in section 104, the following: "the Council on Environmental Quality (established by Public Law 91-190)".

(7) By substituting for "(hereinafter referred to as the 'Committee')", in section 201, the following: "(hereinafter referred to as the 'Citizens' Committee')".

(8) By substituting for the term "the Committee", wherever it occurs, the following: "the Citizens' Committee".

RICHARD NIXON

THE WHITE HOUSE,
March 5, 1970.

(F.R. Doc. 70-2861; Filed, Mar. 5, 1970; 2:29 p.m.)

APPENDIX H

CONSERVATION PERIODICALS

Audubon
published monthly by National Audubon Society, 1130 Fifth Avenue, New York, New York 10028.

BioScience
published monthly by the American Institute of Biological Sciences, 3900 Wisconsin Avenue, N.W., Washington, D.C. 20016.

C. F. Letter
published monthly by The Conservation Foundation, 1717 Massachusetts Avenue, N.W., Washington, D.C. 20036.

Environment
published monthly by the Committee for Environmental Information, 438 North Skinker Boulevard, St. Louis, Missouri 63130.

Environmental Action Newsletter
published bi-weekly by Environmental Action, Inc., 2000 "P" Street, N.W., Washington, D.C. 20036.

Living Wilderness
published quarterly by The Wilderness Society, 729 15th Street, N.W., Washington, D.C. 20005.

National Wildlife
published bimonthly by the National Wildlife Federation, 1412 16th Street, N.W., Washington, D.C. 20036.

Natural History
published monthly by American Museum of Natural History, Central Park West and 79th Street, New York, New York.

Nature
published weekly by Macmillan (Journals) Limited, Little Essex Street, London, W. C. 2, England.

Outdoor America
published monthly by the Izaak Walton League of America, 1326 Waukegan Road, Glenview, Illinois 60025.

Science
published weekly by the American Association for the Advancement of Science, 1515 Massachusetts Avenue, N. W., Washington, D. C. 20005.

Scientific American
published monthly by Scientific American, Inc., 415 Madison Avenue, New York, New York 10017.

Sierra Club Bulletin
published monthly by the Sierra Club, 1050 Mills Tower, San Francisco, California 94104.

BIBLIOGRAPHY

Selected Books and Reports

American Chemical Society. Committee on Chemistry and Public Affairs. Subcommittee on Environmental Improvement. Cleaning our environment: the chemical basis for action. Washington, 1969. 249 p.

Blough, Roy. Regulatory effects of taxation. In his The Federal taxing process. New York, Prentice-Hall, Inc., 1952. pp. 409-26.

Bowen, Howard R. Collective choice. In his Toward social economy. New York, Rinehart and Company, Inc., 1948, pp. 172-198.

Ewald, William R. Environment and policy; the next fifty years. Commissioned and edited by William R. Ewald, Jr. Bloomington, Indiana University Press (c1968) xiv, 459 p. illus.

Galbraith, John Kenneth. The theory of social balance; and The redress of balance. In his the affluent society. Boston, Houghton Mifflin Co., 1958, ch. XVIII, XXII.

National Academy of Engineering Environmental Studies Group. Institutions for effective management of the environment, part I. Washington, 1970. 62 p.

National Air Pollution Control Administration. U. S. Dept. of Health, Education, and Welfare, Guidelines for the Development of Air Quality Standards and Implementation Plans 53 (1969).

Perry, John, 1914-
    Our polluted world: can man survive?, by John Perry.
New York, F. Watts. (c1967) 213 p.

Rienow, Robert, 1907-
    Moment in the sun; a report on the deteriorating quality
of the American environment (by) Robert Rienow and Leona
Train Rienow. New York, Dial Press, 1967. 286 p.

Stepp, J. The pollution problem, by J. M. Stepp and H. H. Ma-
    caulay. Washington, American Enterprise Institute for Pub-
    lic Policy Research (1968) iii, 67 p. 26 cm. (90th Congress,
    second session. Analysis no. 16).

Task Force on Environmental Health and Related Problems. U.S.
    Dept. of Health, Education, and Welfare, A Strategy for a
    Livable Environment 90 (1967).

Selected Law Review Articles

"A Summary of the Right of a Riparian to Pollute a Stream Under
    the New York Common Law." 10 Buffalo Law Review 473
    (1961).

"Air Pollution as a Private Nuisance." 23 Washington & Lee Law
    Review 314 (1967).

Allison and Mann, "The Trial of a Water Pollution Case." 13 Bay-
    lor Law Review 199 (1961).

Barry, "The Evolution of the Enforcement Provisions of the Fed-
    eral Water Pollution Control Act: A Study of the Difficulty in
    Developing Effective Legislation." 68 Michigan Law Review
    1103 (1970).

Baxter, "The SST: From Harlem to Watts in Two Hours." 21
    Stanford Law Review 253 (1969).

"Cold Facts on Hot Water: Legal Aspects of Thermal Pollution."
    Wisconsin Law Review 253 (1969).

Comment, "Air Pollution." 30 University of Pittsburgh Law Review 633 (1969).

Comment, "Air Pollution: Causes, Sources and Abatement." 2 Washington University Law Quarterly 205 (1968).

Comment, "The Conservationists and the Public Lands: Administrative and Judicial Remedies Relating to the Use and Disposition of the Public Lands Administered by the Department of the Interior." 68 Michigan Law Review 1200 (1970).

"Commercial Feedlots--nuisance, zoning and regulation." 6 Washburn Law Journal 493 (1967).

Davis, "Liberalized Law of Standing." University of Chicago Law Review 450 (1970).

Fleming, "Aircraft Noise: a taking of private property without just compensation." 18 Southern California Law Review 593 (1966).

Grady, "Effluent Charges and the Industrial Water Pollution Problem." New England Law Review 61 (1969).

Greenwald, "Law of Noise Pollution." Monograph No. 2. Environment Reporter, May 1, 1970.

Hanks & Hanks, "An Environmental Bill of Rights: The Citizen Suit and the National Environment Policy Act of 1969." 24 Rutgers Law Review 230 (1970).

Hildebrand, "Noise Pollution: An Introduction to the Problem and an Outline for Future Legal Research." 70 Columbia Law Review 652 (1970).

"Landowner's liability to persons outside his premises." 32 Tennessee Law Review 440 (1965).

Martin & Symington, "A Guide to the Air Quality Act of 1967." Law & Contemporary Problems 239 (1968).

Miller & Borchers, "Private Lawsuits and Air Pollution Control."
56 American Bar Association Journal 465 (1970).

"Private Remedies for Water Pollution." 70 Columbia Law Review
734 (1970).

Prosser, "Private Action for Public Nuisance." 52 Virginia Law
Review 997 (1966).

Rodgers, "Persistent Problem of the Persistent Resticides: A Les-
son in Environmental Law." 70 Columbia Law Review 567
(1970).

Sax, "The Public Trust Doctrine in Natural Resource Law: Effective Judicial Intervention." 68 Michigan Law Review 471
(1970).

Scalia, "Sovereign Immunity and Nonstatutory Review of Federal
Administrative Action. Some Conclusions from the Public-
Lands Cases." 68 Michigan Law Review 867 (1970).

Sive, "Some Thoughts of an Environmental Lawyer in the Wilderness of Administrative Law." 70 Columbia Law Review 612
(1970).

Sive, "Securing, Examining and Cross-examining Expert Witnesses in Environmental Cases." 68 Michigan Law Review
1175 (1970).

Spater, "Noise and the Law." 63 Michigan Law Review 1373 (1965).

Sweeney, "Oil Pollution of the Oceans." 37 Fordham Law Review
155 (1968).

Williams, "Legal Techniques to Protect and to Promote Aesthetics
Along Transportation Corridors." 17 Buffalo Law Review 701
(1968).

Note: The publication materials of the Environmental Law Reporter (The Bureau of National Affairs, Inc., Washington,
D.C.) is the most essential and valuable working tool for
professional work in the field of environmental law.

INDEX